I wish I'd said that!

MY FAVORITE AD-LIBS OF ALL TIME

Books by Art Linkletter

PEOPLE ARE FUNNY

KIDS SAY THE DARNDEST THINGS

THE SECRET WORLD OF KIDS

CONFESSIONS OF A HAPPY MAN

KIDS STILL SAY THE DARNDEST THINGS

KIDS SURE RITE FUNNY

A CHILD'S GARDEN OF MISINFORMATION

OOPS!

I WISH I'D SAID THAT!

ART LINKLETTER

I wish I'd said that!

My Favorite Ad-Libs
of All Time

Illustrated by Phil Interlandi

Doubleday & Company, Inc.

GARDEN CITY, NEW YORK

1968

Contents

Foreword: "Off the Cuff"

AD-LIBS are remembered, treasured, and fondly quoted whenever show people get together. They are the quick-on-the-draw remarks that make us sigh, "I wish *I'd* said that!"

But ad-libs are certainly not a special monopoly of show business. These spur-of-the-moment gems crop up in every walk of life, in every epoch, in all kinds of situations—the more dignified, stately, and pompous the occasion, the funnier the result.

After thirty-five years of appearing before audiences of every kind and size, I firmly believe that an off-the-cuff remark, when genuinely spontaneous and unplanned, can set off twice the belly laugh and three times the applause caused by the most carefully prepared "set" gag routine.

In my interviews with kids on my own "House Party" series for the past quarter century, we have been privy to the ad-libs of innocent babes—as pure, unbridled, and unabashed as the bucking of a wild bronco. Their candid remarks about parents have caused more families to move away and relocate under different names than anything since the Oklahoma Land Rush. Their priceless answers could (and did) fill a book.

One of my all-time favorites was the answer to this question: "How did your folks meet and fall in love?"

A five-year-old brightly replied, "I don't know how they met or anything. All I know is they were roommates in college."

A similar question had to do with what parents do for fun. To this query, a puzzled little girl answered, "I don't know because they always lock the door."

The thoughts of children are so delightful. The vast gulf between their world and ours is a refreshingly funny one, and a reminder that most of us have forgotten the magic of things . . . the wonder all around us.

For example, when I advise a child that "we are here on earth to help others," it's only logical that the child's immediate response is: "Then what are the others here for?"

When I teased a youngster with the old riddle, "Which came first, the chicken or the egg?" he indignantly proclaimed, "The chicken, of course. God couldn't lay an egg!"

On one occasion, we were discussing nursery rhymes and what they taught us, and a happy youngster told me that his favorite was "Jack be nimble, Jack be quick." He further explained that he had learned from this never to jump over a candlestick when you have on a nightgown, or you might burn something important!

Good manners came in for a quick, succinct wrap-up by a four-year-old who stated authoritatively, "If you're riding in a car and you're going to throw up . . . do it on yourself!"

The short ad-libs sometimes deliver the weightiest punch:

"What do you want to be when you grow up?"

"Alive!"

"You say you're a normal boy. Do you know what normal means?"

"Yes—ninety-eight point six."

"You don't know your right from your left?"

"No, but I know my front from my back!"

Pets come in for their share of conversation, and youngsters exhibit a strange mixture of wisdom and ignorance, of passion and compassion, when it comes to these furry or fishy members of the family.

"Does your dog have a pedigree?"

"I don't think so. We tried it with the neighbor's dog

for a month and nothing happened."

"Does your cat have a pedigree?"
"We had it cut off last month."

Of course, we grownups manage to get off some spontaneous side-splitters, too. I've been having a wonderful time and making a fine living out of this business of ad-libbing, and encouraging others to ad-lib, for decades. "People Are Funny" rode the NBC airwaves fifty-two weeks a year for twenty years. "House Party" has been in the top five daytime shows on all networks five days a week, fifty-two weeks a year for twenty-five years. "Hollywood Talent Scouts," "Who's Dancing Tonight," "What Do You Think," and many, many more radio and TV shows have kept me busy before the microphones for longer than I sometimes care to think about. But since most of it has been unrehearsed, catch-as-catch-can conversation with all kinds of unusual and interesting people, I look forward to my work each day with the same enthusiasm that I had at the start. I have learned that no matter how disastrous the occasion or unnerving the situation, a frank, honest ad-lib can clear up the mess.

I remember a time when I was to speak at the dedication of a multimillion-dollar hotel: the public-address system was stuttering and whining all through the toastmaster's inroduction. In exasperation, I acknowledged the applause with this remark: "Isn't it amazing how they can spend fourteen million dollars building this gorgeous hotel, and then budget seven dollars and thirty-five cents for a public-address system." It was ludicrous, but it was substantially true—and that's the bottom line for any good ad-lib.

The cut-and-dried formality of a planned program of any kind is always enlivened by an unexpected event that puts the speaker on the spot. The audience waits to see how he's going to "field" the challenge, and even the weakest crack will get an appreciative response. If it's a truly good ad-lib, it will be the high spot of the evening, no matter what else has been set up.

I had asked an audience of forty-five hundred people in McCormick Place in Chicago to rise and salute the flag. A hush fell over the crowded dining room. At just that moment, a prolonged, reverberating crash occurred backstage, as some waiter fell with a large tray full of dishes. When the noise subsided, I turned to the waiting audience and ad-libbed: "The termites holding up the building must have unlocked their arms to salute along with us."

Maybe not too funny in black and white on this page, but it was worth a forty-second laugh in the hall that night.

I have been the toastmaster at thousands of dinners, banquets, retirement affairs, convention meetings, and expositions all over America. I know from long experience that most people go to most banquets expecting to be bored by most of the program, and they relish anything that promises unrehearsed ad-lib fun. One of the dullest political meetings I ever attended was finally rescued when, following a long and boring introduction of another party hack, the public-address system miraculously picked up the wavelength of a nearby radio station, and this announcement came crackling out of the loudspeaker: "Now's the time to put in your spring supply of fertilizer!"

That was the supreme ad-lib. It was delivered anonymously, out of context, and unexpectedly, at exactly the right moment and in precisely the right place!

This book is a collection of my favorite ad-libs of all time. Some of them are culled from backstage bull sessions about show business. Others were jotted down as I read or heard about unexpected flashes of wit in other walks of life —politics, sports, religion, the arts.

I want to thank my old friends, Charlie Rice, author of the "Punchbowl" column in *This Week* Magazine, and Leslie Lieber, Roving Editor of that magazine, for their editorial guidance in compiling this book.

I also want to thank my many friends in show business and other professions, who have helped to swell the collection with their own favorites. The evenings at Danny Thomas' home with people like Joey Bishop, Sheldon

Leonard, Doris Day, the late Nat "King" Cole, and others were rich with ancedotes of this kind. The hours on the dais of the Masquers Club and the Friars in Hollywood with people like George Jessel, Pat Buttram, Frank Sinatra, Bob Hope, Jack Benny, and Steve Allen . . . the fun with Jack Paar on his "Tonight Show," and subsequent evenings with Johnny Carson, Joey Bishop, and two fast-rising young ad-libbers, Merv Griffin and Mike Douglas . . . the excitement of matching quips with Milton Berle, Buddy Hackett, and Don Rickles . . . the smart repartee of Carl Reiner, the prickly jabs of my good friend Groucho Marx, the quicksilver mind of "Fat Jack" Leonard, and the sneaky punch lines of George Burns—all these have sharpened my taste for great ad-lib humor.

I met the very original humorist Fred Allen in his twilight years. But not too late to remind him of a line I once heard him use that epitomizes the classic art of the ad-lib. During one of his mock-serious duels with Jack Benny, Allen was ridiculing Benny's dependence on a large stable of gag writers. In an inspired moment, Fred delivered this wholly spontaneous and absolutely un-toppable *coup de grâce*: "Jack Benny couldn't ad-lib a belch after a Hungarian dinner!"

The Curtain Rises

PURE ad-libs—that is, the kind that are actually generated onstage—are rather hard to come by. Or maybe I should say that uncomplicated ones are scarce, for most of them depend on backstage chitchat. Here are a few that need no explanation—ad-libs that are in the grand tradition of Sir Herbert Beerbohm Tree's retort when he was playing in *King Richard III*. "A horse! My kingdom for a horse!" he cried.

A cutup in the peanut gallery yelled, "Would a jackass do?"

"Certainly," quoth Sir Herbert. "Come down and present yourself."

In 1926, Groucho Marx was playing in *The Coconuts* at the National Theater in Washington, and President Calvin Coolidge made one of his rare visits to the playhouse. The whole cast was abuzz with the event—the President of the United States was right there in the third row!

Groucho behaved as long as he could. But shortly after the second-act curtain rose, he stopped right in the middle of a comedy song, loped to the footlights, and said, "Calvin, aren't you up beyond your bedtime?"

Frank ("Harvey") Fay is thought by many to have been the greatest of night-club ad-libbers. A friend of mine claims to have been present at Broadway's old French Casino when

Fay pulled one of his classics. At a moment's lull in Fay's routine, a drunk hollered, "Ah, you stink!"

Fay drew himself up and said stiffly, "Have a care, sir; you are speaking of the man I love!"

Some years ago when Steve Allen was making a guest appearance on an NBC program, the master of ceremonies asked him if it was really true that he wore a toupee. Said Allen, "No, the hair is real—it's the head that's fake."

Winston Churchill's most dramatic and least-known ad-lib occurred during his broadcast of June 4, 1940, after the Dunkirk disaster. It is least-known because it never was heard by the audience.

The Dean of Canterbury was sitting next to Churchill and he tells of his own deep emotion at hearing the words: "We shall fight on the beaches, we shall fight on the landing grounds, we shall fight in the fields and in the streets!"

"Mr. Churchill put his hand over the microphone," reports the Dean, "and in an aside to me he said with a smile: 'And we will hit them over the head with beer bottles, which is all we have really got.' "

Thank God for the beer bottles—they did the job!

Gerald F. Lieberman is a zany journalist who brags about the number of times he's been fired. Once he appeared on the Jack Paar Show and coined an ad-lib that has been swiped by at least two dozen comedians. Paar asked him, "What do you do for a living?"

Lieberman paused for a moment and replied, "I've been out of work so long, I can't remember."

Smack in the middle of an Oscar Levant performance of Gershwin's pyrotechnic "Piano Concerto in F," in a small college auditorium, the audience became aware of a telephone ringing in an office just offstage. Levant ignored the annoying jangle as his fingers flew over the keyboard, but finally took advantage of a slightly pianissimo passage to turn to the audience and say, without missing a note, "If that's for me, tell them I'm busy."

In accepting an award for his humanitarian work, after a flowery introduction, Jack Benny said, "I don't deserve this, but I have arthritis and I don't deserve that either."

The musical comedy *Jumbo* was the last extravaganza produced at the old Hippodrome Theatre in New York. It is now remembered only for Dick Rodgers' lovely tune, "My Romance," and for a great gag by Jimmy Durante. The story is that the gag was an ad-lib during rehearsal, and it broke everyone up to such an extent that they kept it in the show.

Jumbo was the tale of a struggling circus. When the sheriff came to foreclose, Jimmy Durante grabbed an elephant by the trunk and tried to run off with him. At dress rehearsal, the sheriff yelled to Durante, "Hey, what are you doing with that elephant?"

Durante dropped the beast's trunk and stared in wide-eyed innocence: "What elephant?"

Here is another example of a funny line in a comedian's routine that had its start as a private ad-lib. Press agent

Dick Maney told me that he was once standing in the wings of the New Amsterdam Theatre with Will Rogers during a gorgeous show-girl number of the *Follies*.

"They've certainly got a beautiful bunch of girls in this edition," said Maney.

"Yup," drawled Rogers. "And ain't it sad to think that twenty years from now they'll all be five years older!"

Will later incorporated the gag into his act, and today you will find it reprinted in several anthologies.

Will was a superb ad-libber in every department. He was once toastmaster at a charity luncheon, and there were so many important speakers that a time limit of five minutes had to be imposed. One speaker droned on for nearly half an hour and finally said, "I am sorry, Mr. Toastmaster, that I went beyond the limit, but I left my watch at home."

Said Will, "Don't you even have a pocket calendar?"

Dear old Dizzy Dean, a great pitcher and a great sports announcer, is famous for his "mad-lib" when he signed off a broadcast one day with the cryptic exhortation, "So long, fans—don't fail to miss tomorrow's game."

Another true and fascinating ad-lib can be chalked up for him when he was broadcasting a game during World War II. At the time, it was against defense security rules for a radio announcer to make any mention of the weather. It was thought that Japanese monitors might profit by such details.

Anyway, Diz was broadcasting a game, and in the sixth inning the umpires stopped play because of a sudden downpour. Diz reported, "Folks, the game has been called temporarily. I ain't allowed to tell you why, but if you're curious, just stick your head out the window."

Tallulah Bankhead often feuded with her leading men. (She'd be the first to admit it.) Once, during the Broadway run of a drawing-room comedy, Tallu hatched a great scheme: she charmed an assistant stage manager into ringing the telephone bell in the middle of her leading man's greatest speech. She knew he would be near the telephone and could not ignore it.

The plot worked out beautifully. Just as the leading man was at the climax of his lines, the phone started ringing. At first he tried to drown it out with a burst of fortissimo. But it kept ringing, and he finally succumbed. He picked up the receiver and murmured a limp "Hello." Suddenly, a gleam of desperate genius lighted his eyes. He turned to Tallulah and extended the receiver: "It's for *you,* my dear."

One night back in 1894, George Bernard Shaw turned up for the first-night performance of his *Arms and the Man.* As the final curtain fell, the audience applauded wildly and the author himself came out to take a bow. The general acclaim was broken by the sound of one lone hiss emanating from one of the last rows.

Shaw held up his hands for silence. Then he lifted his eyes towards the balcony and said, "I agree with you, sir. But what can we two do against so many?"

The Curtain Falls

It is after the show that most actors really get going and spout better lines than playwrights ever wrote for them. My favorite ones below were chosen from several hundred, but perhaps none will quite equal the classic line that Rex Harrison uttered when he stopped before a fish market and observed the rows of flounders staring up at him with glazed eyes. "My God," he said with a shudder, "it's like Wednesday matinée in Philadelphia!"

Barbra Streisand had finished a matinée of *Funny Girl* at the Winter Garden and was leaving the stage door. A group of three polite teen-age girls announced that they were loyal fans from Brooklyn and would like to present her with a gift. Whereupon they solemnly unfolded a colorful bolero jacket *woven entirely of chewing-gum wrappers.*

Miss Streisand was thunderstruck. When she finally could speak, she gasped, "You mean you chewed all that gum for *me?*"

Back in the days when Charlie Chaplin called America his home, he was entertaining friends at a Hollywood party by giving imitations of famous performers. When he launched into an operatic aria, coming through on key and in crystal-clear tones, an astonished guest sidled up and said, "Why, Charlie, I didn't know you could sing."

"I can't," Charlie answered. "I'm just imitating Caruso."

Joe Frisco was noted for his gambling as well as for his gags and his stuttering. One day when he was roaming forlorn around the grandstand at Santa Anita Racetrack, he ran into friend, Bing Crosby, from whom he cadged one hundred dollars. The horse he bet on won and paid off 7 to 1. That night, Frisco was treating a group of his pals to drinks and dinner at a ritzy restaurant when Bing Crosby passed the table. Grabbing him by the elbow, Frisco grandiloquently peeled a one-hundred-dollar bill from his bankroll and said, "Here, k-k-kid, sing us something."

Bob Hope was having a skull-session with some of his gag writers, and said that he'd run across a pretty funny gag that might be worked into his upcoming script.

"But, Bob, you can't use that," said one of the gag writers. "I heard Jack Paar use that one just the other night."

"You're right," said Bob. "It wouldn't be fair to offer Red Skelton thirdhand material."

20

Carol Channing and *Hello, Dolly!* became so famous an American tradition that, at one publicity party, even the *National Geographic* Magazine sent photographers. Carol was amazed and elated. When the *National Geographic* cameras were set up to take pictures of her, she burbled, "Which do you want, my north, south, east, or west?"

Bea Lillie was giving a small dinner party at her East Side apartment, when suddenly there was a flutter at the open window. A stray pigeon had landed on the ledge and was eying the group curiously.

"Oh, hello," piped Bea. "Any messages?"

Some hot-off-the-griddle remarks have such sparkle that they go down in history as book titles. Hearken, for instance, to the deathless ad-lib of the great Viennese tenor, Leo Slezak. One night the irrepressible Slezak was singing in *Lohengrin,* in which the tenor always makes a triumphal exit on a huge swan, which is hauled offstage by a rope. But this night, the stagehands missed their cue and started pulling too soon. Slezak finished his aria, looked around for the swan and saw it disappearing into the wings. He was stunned—but not speechless. Turning to the audience, he shrugged his shoulders in helplessness and called out, "What time does the next swan leave?"

That ad-lib was later selected by actor Walter Slezak, son of Leo, as the title to his best-selling book of reminiscences.

Another ad-lib that later became a book title was hatched one day when comedian Joe Frisco visited a stockbroker's office on the zillionth floor of a Wall Street skyscraper. The broker proudly showed Joe the panorama of New York bay, and pointed out half a dozen yachts that belonged to big-shot brokers.

"Great," said Joe. "But where are the *customers'* yachts?"

Henny Youngman, who bills himself as "The King of the One-Liners," was having what he thought was a serious conversation about smoking with ad-librettist friend, Milton Berle. "Do you inhale, Milton?" asked Henny solicitously.

"Not while you're in the room, I don't," said Berle.

Incidentally, before Berle became a famous TV star, he was noted for collecting other comedians' gags. One day in the mid-thirties, an agent walked into Dinty Moore's restaurant and announced to the faithful at the bar, "Hey, did you hear that Milton Berle had to cancel out at the Palace? He broke his ankle."

Said Lou Holtz, "He must have fallen off his files."

22

Fred Allen, in his vaudeville days, was booked for eight weeks in Western Canada, in the dead of winter. When he finally managed to mush back to the Lambs Club, he unbosomed his woes to a group of friends. "Manitoba is the end of everything," he said. "Sixteen below zero. We had to play four shows on weekdays and five shows on Saturday."

"Five!" gasped a listener. "But how did they clear the customers between shows?"

"Oh," said Fred, "they just opened the back doors and let the wolves run through."

23

One of the most improbable comedy teams ever assembled was Jimmy Durante and soprano Helen Traubel. They were a glorious fixture on many a TV show.

One night Jimmy ventured backstage at the Metropolitan Opera for the first time in his life. He made his way to Miss Traubel's dressing room, and was thunderstruck to encounter her in the formidable armor costume that she wore as Brunhilde in *Tannhäuser*.

"Holy smoke!" he gasped. "You've been *drafted!*"

One of the most charming ad-libs I can remember was also made by Jimmy Durante. I visited him some years ago in the suite which was constantly reserved for him at the Astor Hotel. I have never in my life seen a hotel suite more infested with friends: some coming, some leaving— always a parade.

The phone rang, and Eddie Jackson answered. "Hey, Jimmie, there's a guy named Dave Rappaport from Jersey City down in the lobby. Do you know him?"

"Never hoid of him. You ever hoid of him?"

"Nope," said Eddie. "Hey, everybody, quiet down for a second. Has anybody heard of Dave Rappaport from Jersey City?"

Everyone drew a blank.

"So nobody ever hoid of him," said Jimmie. "Ah, what the hell, tell him to come on up anyway."

For all his gentle nature, Lucien Guitry could be most severe in matters theatrical. Once, when he was directing a play, he was dissatisfied with the entrance of a minor actor: "Monsieur, please try to make your entrance with greater dignity."

The nervous actor tried again, and this time he entered with a ridiculous spraddle-legged stride. "Monsieur," cried Guitry, "I asked you to enter with dignity, not on horseback!"

24

What is there to say about W. C. Fields? Where is one to begin? One of my favorites is his remark to a panhandler who approached him on Broadway, near the Astor Hotel. "Sorry, my good man," intoned The Genius, "but all my money is tied up in currency."

Corey Ford, an old friend of Fields, reports a few that are new to me. Once, explaining his drinking habits, Fields said, "I make it a practice to keep a reasonable supply of medicinal stimulants on hand, in case I encounter a venomous snake—which I also keep on hand."

Once when Corey asked him how he judged when he'd had enough to drink, The Great Man thought for a moment. "When my knees start to bend backwards."

Fields had little use for the big shots of Hollywood. One day Corey answered the phone and clapped his hand over the mouthpiece. "It's Louis B. Mayer," he whispered to

Fields. "He wants to know why you didn't show up for the first day of shooting on the new picture."

"Give him an evasive answer," said Fields. "Something on the order of 'Drop dead.' "

Sir William Gilbert, the lyricist in the immortal light-opera writing team of Gilbert and Sullivan, was noted for his sour nature and ill-concealed temper. An actor who had often felt the whiplash of Gilbert's vituperation asked him one day how he was.

"Just so-so," replied Gilbert. "It's indigestion, I fancy, but I have a peculiarly bitter taste in my mouth."

"Been biting your tongue?" cracked the player of bit parts.

The late Gertrude Lawrence was one of those irreplaceables who seldom had an understudy. If she was sick, the show was off. An aspiring actress discovered this, to her dismay, when she auditioned before Moss Hart for a part in a play he was producing. She announced that, among her other credits, she had been the understudy in *Susan and God,* one of Miss Lawrence's great hits.

"Interesting," murmured Hart. "I take it you were understudying God?"

Here's an ad-lib hatched by the famous Hungarian playwright, Ferenc Molnár, which might come in handy for many of us weak-willed moderns who are too quick to accept free invitations. Molnár and friend found themselves with two free tickets to a Budapest play. Early in the insufferable first act, Molnár got up to leave.

"You can't walk out," objected his companion. "We're guests of the management."

Molnár meekly sat down, but after a few more doses of insipid dialogue, he arose again.

"Now where are you going?" queried his friend.

"I'm going to the box office to buy two tickets so we can leave," said Molnár.

Sarah Bernhardt was certainly the greatest toast of the town that Paris ever boasted. One night at the theater, a new callboy tapped reverently at her dressing-room door and said, "Madame, it will be eight o'clock when it suits you."

Madame Sarah rushed to the door and gave the young gallant a kiss. From then on, it was tradition for all callboys, in every theater that she played, to give the warning, "Madame, it will be eight o'clock when it suits you."

Heaven, Inc.

THE CLERGY and matters religious are always a rich source of quips, possibly because the Church is a celestial branch of show business. So let us take our text today from the famed remark of George Bernard Shaw, who, when asked by a rector's wife which denomination he belonged to, exploded, "Madam, I am an atheist, and I thank God for it!"

During the Brooklyn Dodgers-New York Yankees World Series of 1953, Cardinal Spellman put in an appearance in a front-row box along the third-base line. A high foul ball came in his direction with Dodger catcher Roy Campanella in hot but fruitless pursuit. The ball bounced on the railing and caromed onto the noted churchman's knee. Campanella took a split second off to enquire respectfully if Cardinal Spellman had been hurt.

"Don't worry about me, Roy," said His Eminence. "God had the wisdom to make a priest's knees the toughest part of his anatomy."

Wilton Lackaye, a famous American actor of the gaslight era, was once present at a banquet where the minister who was supposed to say grace failed to show up. Lackaye, asked at the last minute to fill the bill, arose, lowered his head reverently, and said, "There being no clergyman present, let us thank God."

Television and radio star Garry Moore once received an award for his spontaneity. In accepting it, he graciously paid tribute to "the four guys responsible for my spontaneity—my writers."

The next to receive an award was Bishop Fulton J. Sheen. He stepped up to the microphone and with characteristic good humor announced, "I also want to pay tribute to *my* four writers—Matthew, Mark, Luke, and John."

When Horace Greeley, militant editor of the New York *Tribune,* wasn't telling young men to go West he was telling them someplace else where they could head in. One day a man came up to him soliciting funds for missionary work "to save millions of your fellow creatures from going to hell."

Said Horace Greeley, "I won't give you a damned cent. There don't half enough of them go now."

Lewis Browne, famous author of *This Believing World* and other best sellers on the religions of mankind, was a rabbi before he opted for the pen. One day at a literary dinner, a wary rabbi gave Browne the third degree about his theological beginnings. "So you were a rabbi?" he asked. "Were you defrocked?"

"No," answered Browne, "just unsuited."

Dr. S. Parkes Cadman, pioneer radio preacher, was once asked by a young listener whether it was possible to lead a good Christian life in New York City on eighteen dollars a week.

"My boy," replied Dr. Cadman, "that's all you *can* do."

My old friend Horace McNabb, press agent extraordinary, tells about one spring when he was traveling north with the New York Yankees on their spring-training tour. In Memphis, Casey Stengel made the astounding announcement: "I hafta phone a nunnery." It seems that his wife, Edna, had a friend in a local seminary, and Casey had promised to get in touch with her.

So Casey called and said, "Sister Angela? This is Casey Stengel, manager of the New York Yankees."

"Who?"

"Casey Stengel—Edna's husband."

"Oh, of course! . . . And what is it you said you do?"

"I'm manager of the Yankees."

"Manager?"

"Yeah—you know what I mean. I'm sorta the Mother Superior."

Cecil B. DeMille, who rivaled Moses as a popularizer of the Ten Commandments, was once asked by a fellow producer why he had turned out so many movies based on the Bible. Answered DeMille, "Why let two thousand years of publicity go to waste?"

A Boston parishioner, seeking to impress Cardinal Richard Cushing with his piety, was bemoaning the fact that there seem to be so few saints among us in this crass twentieth century.

"Well let's all give thanks for that," said the eminent Cardinal. "Saints are all right in heaven, but they're hell on earth."

The late Pope John, shortly after his accession, was asked to examine the preliminary design for his papal coat of arms. With great fanfare, a large scroll of paper was rolled out on his desk. Pope John studied it and said gently, "Please don't make my lion look so cross."

The mother of Edna St. Vincent Millay liked to tell about a time when the poet was a little girl. One day she rushed down the stairs and cried, "Mummy, I just saw an elephant in the back yard." Mrs. Millay sighed; she was becoming a bit alarmed about Edna's vivid imagination. "Edna, you really mustn't tell so many fibs; it was probably only that big dog next door. Now, I think you should go up to your room and ask God to forgive you."

Edna went upstairs, and when she reappeared a few minutes later, Mrs. Millay asked, "Did you do as I told you?"

"Yes, Mummy. And God said, 'Don't worry, Edna—for a minute *I* thought it was an elephant too.' "

Napoleon Bonaparte was far from a model of piety. Once when one of his ministers brought up the question of government support for certain convents, he said, "I don't really have anything against convents—but I wish they wouldn't admit any women under fifty."

At about the same time, Sophie Arnould, famed French singer, expressed the notion a bit more cruelly. When she heard that a fading Parisian beauty was about to take the veil, she said, "Women give themselves to God when the Devil wants nothing more to do with them."

When the great W. C. Fields was mortally ill, his friend Gene Fowler dropped in on him and caught him reading the Bible. Fowler was astounded—Fields had never found any use for a Bible other than to prop up a martini. Fowler said, "Bill, I'm deeply touched——"

"Don't bother," muttered Fields. "I'm only looking for loopholes."

The Spouse of Life

PERHAPS the definitive critique on the institution of matrimony was written by an unknown schoolboy on an examination paper: "The Christian religion allows a man to have only one wife. This system is called monotony."

A more valid ad-lib, almost as well-known, is credited to Oliver Wendell Holmes: One night he arrived home quite late, and his wife called down the stairs, "Is that you Oliver!"

He replied, "Yes, my dear—whom were you expecting!"

Well, it just goes to show that marriage is not necessarily monotony, and my supply of ad-libs about the little woman almost runneth over!

Bea Lillie was once matron of honor at the wedding of a lady friend. The minister began ticking off the traditional nuptial obligations: "Do you, Mary, promise faithfully . . . for as long as ye both shall live . . . forsaking all others . . ."

Miss Lillie almost broke up the ceremony by murmuring, "Oh, dear, that sounds tighter than a Shubert contract!"

During the 1964 Presidential campaign, Hubert Humphrey delivered a long, important speech in a Midwest city, and afterward received the acclaim and handshakes of a host of friends. When he approached his wife, Muriel, for approbation, she said, "Hubert, to be eternal you don't have to be endless."

When a reporter, pencil at the alert, news nose aquiver, and expectations high, asked French authoress and existentialist, Françoise Sagan, for a comment on her wedding, she huffed, "I said 'Yes.' Isn't that enough?"

One of the best marital ad-libs I ever heard was told me by Dr. Cyril ("Chuck") Solomon, of New York. One night, he said, he was awakened by a frantic call from an old friend who beseeched him to rush to the aid of his wife. "She's having an acute case of appendicitis."

"Nonsense," said Dr. Chuck. "I took your wife's appendix out five years ago. Nobody can have another case of appendicitis."

"Maybe so," yelled the man. "But a guy can have another wife, can't he?"

The wonderful old stage veteran, the late Howard Lindsay, who was the original Father in *Life with Father,* was asked a stock question by a naïve reporter: "Mr. Lindsay, can you remember the best piece of advice that you ever received?"

"Oh, yes," the actor replied with spirit. "It was the time many years ago that I was advised to marry my lovely wife, Dorothy Stickney."

"Sir, do you remember who gave you that advice?"

"Certainly—she did."

Ashley Montagu, in his recent book, *The Anatomy of Swearing,* cited a Mark Twain ad-lib that was new to me (and I thought I knew most of them). One day Twain's strait-laced wife was more than usually upset about his penchant for colorful cursing. As an object lesson, she made him sit down and listen to her repeat a dozen or more curse words that he used in his daily conversation. "Now, how do you think that sounds?" she demanded.

"Well," said Twain thoughtfully, "the words are there, my dear—but the music is wanting."

Jack Benny has always taken pride that his wife, Mary, is an unusually innocent-minded woman. One day Mary started worrying about a dearly loved young cat and called the vet: "I wish you'd drop by and have a look at her. She's getting awfully fat, but I know she can't be having kittens. She's never been out of the house except once in a while on a leash."

The vet called and pronounced the cat pregnant.

"Impossible," said Mary.

Just then another cat stuck its head out from under the living-room sofa. "Ha," said the vet, "that looks like a tomcat to me."

"Well, yes," said Mary, "but he's only her *brother.*"

Maxfield Parrish, the famed illustrator, had spurts of energy for huge frescoes, such as the one in the King Cole Bar at the St. Regis Hotel. But he also had periods of lassitude that worried his family and friends. Parrish specialized in lush nudes, and one morning a lovely young model showed up at his studio to pose.

"I don't feel like working right now," said Parrish. "Let's have a cup of coffee."

No sooner had they sat down than the studio buzzer rang. Parrish answered it and quickly slapped his hand over the transmitter. "Young lady," he cried, "for God's sake, take your clothes off—my wife's coming up to check on me!"

When Mrs. Albert Einstein was asked if she understood her husband's theory of relativity, she answered, "No . . . but I know my husband and I know he can be trusted."

The plump and comfortable Sultan of Shudders, Alfred Hitchcock, often embarrasses his wife by going to sleep at parties. At one posh Hollywood gathering, he corked off for a record two hours, and his wife finally shook him surreptitiously. "I think we'd better go home!" she whispered crossly.

Mr. Hitchcock started, peered at his watch, and murmured, "Go? But it's only twelve-thirty—they'd think we weren't enjoying ourselves."

Long before famed orchestra leader Paul Whiteman became the Dean of Modern American Music he qualified as Dean of America's Fat Men. During his pudgy period Paul put all his heart and weight (345 pounds) into courting and proposing marriage to movie actress Margaret Livingston. Time and time again Pops popped the question, but to no avail. Finally, in desperation, he asked Miss Livingston why she constantly turned him down.

"I will never marry a man I can't put my arms around," sighed Miss Livingston.

P.S. Paul went on a marathon diet and got the girl by a slim margin.

A pretty young American girl went to Paris armed with a letter of introduction to Sacha Guitry, the great French actor. "Mr. Guitry," she said, "I am just dying to make my mark in the theater. Would you listen to me recite, and give me your advice?"

Guitry, always a soft touch for a pretty face, agreed. The young lady recited, the master listened. After the recitation there was a moment of silence. Guitry finally approached the fluttering girl, kissed her on either cheek, and said, "My dear child, marry soon. Good-by."

Wild-Bore Hunting

BORES and boors lead with their chins, so it is natural that they should be a rich mine of ad-libs. I call upon the eloquent G. B. S. again for the topper in this department: Lady None-such once sent him a message reading, "Lady None-such will be at home from 4:30 to 6:30 on Thursday next."

He quickly scribbled his reply: "So will Mr. Shaw."

Comedian Paul Ford, a trusting soul, was lunching one noon with his less trustful friend, Orson Bean. A sharp Broadway producer dropped by the table and discussed a proposition with Ford, and as he left, he said, "You know me, Paul—I'd give you my right arm."

"A real sincere guy!" exclaimed Ford.

"Yeah?" said Bean. "I happen to know that he's got a whole bureau drawer full of right arms."

Which reminds me of an earlier quip made by the late Bobbie Clark. An actor was speaking about a director who was less than well-loved. "He talks pretty mean, but he'd really give you the shirt off his back."

"Yeah?" said Clark. "But who'd wear it!"

George S. Kaufman was at a party one evening when a boring couple rose to make their farewells, and then kept the hostess at the door for twenty minutes in endless leave-taking. Kaufman rolled his eyes to the ceiling and murmured, "God, one of the tragedies of life—forgotten but not gone."

Which leads to another Kaufmanism: In the days of the five-cent telephone call, a number of Broadway wits were gathered at Gallagher's when a particularly loathsome leading man walked in and insisted on joining the party. After a few moments he asked, "Has anybody got a nickel? I have to phone a friend."

George Kaufman flipped him a coin and said, "Here's a dime—phone all of them."

At the Dutch Treat Club, Lowell Thomas ran across a crashing bore who had recently become a member. The bore was livid with rage. "What kind of an organization is this?" he sputtered. "I just overheard a man say he'd give fifty dollars if I resigned."

Mr. Thomas advised, "Hold out for a hundred—you'll get it."

Society has always had its quota of deadly bores. Nowadays business and social hypocrisy — and our heightened sense of tolerance — demands that we smile benignly on them. But in the old days pests were politely told to go jump in the lake.

Alexander Woollcott managed it in a civilized way when he suddenly interrupted a young actor who didn't know when to stop talking. "Excuse me," said the Town Crier, "my leg has gone to sleep. Do you mind if I join it?"

Similarly Charles Lamb, the great English essayist, ran into a long-winded and insipid acquaintance of his on Fleet Street.

"What's going on, Charles?" asked the bore.

"I am," Lamb replied—and did.

Comedian Danny Klayman reminded me of a classic:

Ring Lardner lived for many years on Long Island, and one day when a boring lady neighbor asked him to a party on Friday evening, he replied, "I'm sorry, but it's the children's night out, and I have to stay home with the nurse."

A few years ago, Martin Freud, the son of the great Dr. Sigmund Freud, was interviewed by a reporter who asked too many personal questions about the Freud family life. The younger Freud closed off the subject neatly by remarking, "I didn't know the full facts of life until I was seventeen. My father never talked about his work."

Benjamin Disraeli was an accomplished novelist before he came to fame in the British Government. One day a friend asked him the nineteenth-century equivalent of that sturdy cliché: "Have you read any good books lately?"

Disraeli answered with his usual humility, "When I want to read a book, I write one."

Groucho Marx was lunching at Romanoff's one day and a lady autograph-stalker spotted him. "Oh, dear me," she twittered, "let me think . . . are you Harpo?"

"No, madam," he snapped. "Are you?"

I can think of only one occasion on which Groucho was bested in repartee. The winner, of all people, was Greta Garbo. Groucho once spotted her sitting alone in the Palm Room of the Plaza Hotel. She had on a huge droopy hat, and Groucho couldn't resist a sudden impulse. He sidled up to her, lifted the brim of the hat and peeked under it. "Pardon," he said, "but I thought you were a fellow I met at Sweeney's Bar."

Miss Garbo gave him a glacial stare. "But I am not," she said.

Groucho was flustered for once in his life. Feeling a word of explanation was due, he stammered, "I'm sorry—I'm Groucho Marx."

Miss Garbo continued to stare and said very simply, "That is too bad."

One of the great Sardi ad-libs has been told about countless unbeloved Broadway characters. Currently the target is producer David Merrick, widely known as "The Abominable Showman." Merrick was having lunch with a group of non-admirers, and at dessert time he said, "I think I'll have a bit of cheese."

One of his companions muttered, "With crackers or in a trap?"

A puritanical lady suddenly froze as she looked through her lorgnette at a painting on the wall of Whistler's studio.

"Isn't that picture indecent?" she huffed.

"No, madam," said Whistler, "but your question is."

When Mark Twain was living in Rochester, New York, he visited a neighbor who had an excellent library. Twain asked if he might borrow a certain book.

"I'd be delighted to have you read it here," said the neighbor rather stuffily. "I have had to adopt a rule that books may not leave these premises."

Some weeks later, the neighbor rang Twain's doorbell and asked if he might use his lawn mower. "By all means," said Twain. "But under a recently adopted rule, you must use it on these premises."

Vic Oliver, a brash English comic, for a while happened to be Churchill's son-in-law. One day Oliver airily asked Churchill, "Who do you think was the greatest statesman in World War II?"

"Mussolini," Churchill glowered. "He had the guts to shoot his son-in-law."

The poet Robert Browning was a man of great politeness, as attested by a problem that beset him one night at a London party. A professional pest buttonholed him and rambled on endlessly about his opinions on poetry. After fifteen or twenty minutes, when the bore was physically forced to pause for breath, Browning seized his opportunity: "Fascinating, dear chap. But I must not forget my manners by monopolizing you further."

A misguided garden-club lady got a rather curt turn-down when she tried to soft-soap W. C. Fields into addressing her society's annual banquet. "But surely you believe in clubs for women," said the matron.

"Certainly," said Fields, "but only if all other means of persuasion fail."

That "most-disliked person in show business" keeps bobbing up all over the place, inspiring grumpy ad-libs by the carload. Oscar Levant and some of his cronies were discussing this friendless scalawag at Dinty Moore's one day when one of his unadmirers mused, "I wish somebody would kidnap that guy."

"Swell idea," said Levant. "But who would they contact?"

A lady journalist with much push and no popularity (let us call her Daphne) spotted columnist Irving Hoffman at a Broadway opening. Daphne was intensely interested because Irving was squiring a new girl friend. She rushed up to shake his hand. Said Irving, presenting his girl friend, "Daphne, I want you to say hello and good-by to Miss Jones."

John Barrymore, hardly a self-effacing type of man, was often annoyed when people confused him with his brother Lionel. One day he was ordering some shirts in a Broadway shop, and the clerk asked his name. "Barrymore," he replied haughtily.

The clerk, properly impressed, stammered, "Uh—which one?"

John gave him a frigid glare and said, "*Ethel!*"

Which reminds me that Ethel was no mean hand at ad-libbing. Her friends called her "Eth"—but *only* her friends. One night at an after-theater party, a butter-and-egg man from out West heard several people call her "Eth," so he decided to try it himself. "I've always been one of your faithful fans, Eth," he said.

She eyed him coldly. "Why be so formal?" she remarked. "Just call me Butch."

The Diamond
Is a Boy's Best Friend

THERE'S BEEN a lot of sports-page scuttlebutt that
football may be pushing baseball off its pedestal as
America's national pastime. Off its pedestal, maybe—
but out of our hearts, never! We ad-lib hunters know
that there are more wonderful stories about baseball
than all the other sports put together — even including
golf. What other sport has produced a Hercules of
Humor to match Casey Stengel, whose greatest of many
ejaculations came one day when he was managing the
lowly Mets. In a moment of despair, when he was trying
to figure out the day's line-up, he looked down his bench
and asked, "Is there anybody here that can play this
game?"

In the following selections, you will find several
sports represented, but baseball is the winner.

Yogi Berra, at one time the most voluble as well as the
most valuable player in the American League, was attending a water festival with Mickey Mantle at nearby Tampa
during the Yankees' spring training in Florida. Mantle
pointed to a Jolly Roger flying from the mast of a make-be-
lieve pirate frigate.

"I'll bet you don't know what the skull and crossbones on
that flag means," said Mantle.

"Sure I do," Berra answered. "It means iodine."

In fact Yogi is famous for a thousand unwitting ad-libs, the best-known being his remark at Yankee Stadium on Yogi Berra Day. After accepting several automobiles, matched sets of luggage, and golf clubs, bestowed upon him by loyal fans, he strode to the microphone and said, "I want to thank all you folks for making this day necessary."

But a less well-known ad-lib, and just as unintentional, was born when his manager, Casey Stengel, told him for heaven's sake to think when he went to bat.

Yogi exploded to several teammates: "Jeez, what does he expect—I'm supposed to hit and think too?"

Dear old Tom Meany, the prince of sportswriters, could give you sixty ad-libs to the minute and never miss a swallow of his "Horse's Neck Stiff." Tom claimed to have been on a pre-season exhibition tour with the New York Yankees when the players were booked into a hotel with old-fashioned Murphy beds that folded up into the wall. According to Tom, Yogi (then a rookie) entered his room, took one look around and beefed, "Hey, this is the end! I'm a big-league player—I ain't going to sleep standing up!"

Tom also loved to tell about the day that Babe Ruth spotted a seedy-looking character in the box seats. "That bum's been here for the last four or five games. How can he afford it?"

Tom said, "He's a dear old friend of Colonel Ruppert. He used to be very rich, but the poor guy lost a fortune in the war."

"Yeah?" said the Babe. "What did he do—bet on the Germans?"

The easy-going Willie Mays was recently hired to play "himself" in a TV baseball drama. He arrived at the studio as genial as always, and the director said, "Willie, we know that you're not used to acting. Do you think you'll have any trouble being your natural self?"

"Well, I'll tell you," said Willie. "Just you turn the cameras on, and if it ain't me, lemme know."

Johnny Sain, the great National League pitcher, likes to tell a story about himself when he was a pert young rookie. One afternoon he faced the fabulous Rogers Hornsby for the first time. "I knew he was the greatest hitter of all time, but I figured I could fool him by pitching carefully."

Johnny threw one ball that didn't quite catch the corner of the plate. He threw another, which also missed, according to Umpire Bill Klem. Johnny was getting annoyed, and when Umpire Klem called the next close pitch a ball, Sain walked halfway to the plate and said sarcastically, "Say, Ump, will you let me know when I pitch a strike?"

"Young man," replied Umpire Klem, "when you pitch a strike, Mr. Hornsby will let you know."

The veteran Charlie Grimm was managing the Chicago Cubs one year when they couldn't hit the size of their hats, and thus had sunk deep into the National League cellar. One evening a Chicago Cub scout phoned excitedly from some tank town in Iowa and said, "Boss, I've just stumbled on a great pitching find. This afternoon the kid pitched a *perfect* game. Twenty-seven strike-outs in a row! Nobody even *touched* the ball till a guy hit a foul in the last inning. Listen, Boss, the kid's with me right now. . . . Shall I sign him up?"

"No," Charlie groaned. "Sign up the guy who got the foul—we need hitters."

One afternoon in St. Louis, Stan ("The Man") Musial was having a field day against the Chicago pitcher, crusty "Bobo" Newsome. Stan first slammed a single, then a triple, and then a homer. When Stan came up to bat for the fourth time, the Chicago manager decided to yank "Bobo" and take a chance on a rookie relief pitcher.

The rookie trudged in from the bull pen and took the ball from "Bobo." "Say," he murmured, "has this guy Musial got any weakness?"

"Yeah," grunted "Bobo," "he can't hit doubles."

Which reminds me of another Musial ad-lib. The Pittsburgh Pirates were playing at St. Louis, and Catcher Joe Garagiola was spinning out his usual line of chatter in an effort to distract the Cardinal batters. When Musial stepped up to the plate, Joe said, "Hey, Stan, I understand that restaurant you run is a pretty good place . . ."

A ball whizzed over the plate and Musial missed it.

Encouraged, Joe went on: "Me and some of the guys thought we'd drop in tonight for steak . . ."

Another ball whizzed in—Bam! Musial poled it into the bleachers for a home run. He jogged comfortably around the bases and as he passed home plate, he said: "By the way, Joe, how do you guys like your steaks, rare or medium?"

In a spring exhibition game between the Milwaukee Braves and the New York Yankees, Catcher Yogi Berra was trying to rattle the Braves' star slugger, Hank Aaron. "Hank," he said, "you're holding the bat with the trademark wrong. It should face upward."

The imperturbable Hank just waved the bat.

"Listen," said Yogi, "you're sure as hell gonna split that bat if you don't turn the trademark up."

Hank kept waving away and answered, "Mr. Berra, my manager sent me up here to hit with this bat, not to read it."

Golfer Don January reported a choice ad-lib made by Dutch Harrison during the course of a pro-amateur game Dutch played with a celebrity hacker. When the hacker lodged a tee shot in the high crotch of a tree, he turned affably to the harassed Dutch. "How" he asked, "would you play that?"

"Under an assumed name," said Dutch.

Bing Crosby often tells a story about a priest friend, Father Kelly, who is an enthusiastic but erratic golfer. One day at Pebble Beach, he was advised by his caddie to use a No. 3 iron to reach the green. "I think I can make it with a 'four,'" said Father Kelly. "I'll take a full swing and pray."

He did, and the ball fell short, right in a sand trap. "Guess the good Lord didn't hear me," he sighed.

"Could be," said the caddie. "But in our church, when we pray, we keep our heads down."

Although horse racing is allegedly the sport of kings, Sir Gordon Richards is the first jockey to have been knighted by the British Crown. When five-foot Sir Gordon, who was scarcely obliged to kneel to receive the Queen's sword on his shoulder, first heard of the honor, he quipped, "I never realized that I'd end up being the shortest knight of the year."

Football Coach Mike Holovak tells a story about "Bulldog" Turner, who played center for the Chicago Bears. One evening after an important victory, the Bears were having a party in a Chicago hotel. Festivities reached such a pitch that "Bulldog" tumbled out the window, fell three stories to the sidewalk. He would have been killed if he hadn't fallen through an awning, which broke the impact. As "Bulldog" picked himself up, a policeman charged up and demanded, "All right, now, what's going on?"

Said "Bulldog," "I don't know, officer—I just got here myself."

The late Bill Slocum, colorful sportswriter for the old New York *Journal-American*, was collecting his notes prior to leaving the press box after a ball game. A cub sports reporter, trying to get his bearings after covering his first game in the huge Yankee Stadium, pointed towards the sun setting behind the grandstand. "That's the west, isn't it?" he asked.

"If it isn't," said Slocum, "you've just come up with the scoop of the year."

Musical Depreciation

MUSIC SEEMS to tower over the other arts when it comes to quick wit. For some reason it parallels baseball in its ad-lib ascendancy over other sports. Maybe it's because so many fiddlers have to rub elbows, and often rub them the wrong way.

My special favorite? I think it must be the unwitting ad-lib of a stagehand one night when Koussevitzky was conducting d'Indy's "Mountain Symphony" in Boston. The score calls for an offstage horn passage, to give the effect of an echo from the distance. The horn player took his stance in the wings, dutifully watching Koussevitzky's baton. Just as the player raised the horn to his mouth for his solo, a stagehand rushed up and snatched the instrument from him. "Hey, you can't play that thing here," he whispered. "Don't you know there's a concert going on?"

Arturo Toscanini was famous for scolding musicians whose efforts did not please him. One day during a rehearsal, he got furious at the whole orchestra. He slammed down his baton, wiped his brow in desperation and said very deliberately, "After I die, I shall return to earth as the doorkeeper of a bordello and I won't let a single one of you in!"

Toscanini was rehearsing the New York Philharmonic Orchestra one afternoon when he heard what he deemed a poor passage from trumpeter Harry Glantz. The maestro flew into a rage and delivered a long and fiery volley of insults in Italian. Glantz was too fine a musician to stand for such abuse, so he stalked off in a huff. As Toscanini paused for breath in mid-tirade, Glantz turned and shouted, "Ah, nuts!"

Toscanini raised his hand in majesty and said, "No, no, signor, eet ees too late for apologies!"

Max Herzberg, a collector of scathing remarks made down through the ages, prizes the retort of Wolfgang Amadeus Mozart to a young music student who asked how to write a symphony. Mozart told the ambitious young man to begin with something simple—like ballads.

"But you composed symphonies when you were only ten years old," objected the youth.

"True," replied Mozart, "but I didn't ask how."

The following ad-lib has been attributed to about every music critic and opera manager who ever lived. The late H. T. Parker, critic of the Boston *Transcript,* is very possibly the one who actually said it. When Parker heard that the petite Lily Pons was to make her debut in *Carmen,* he said, "Thank God! At last we'll have a Carmen who weighs less than the bull!"

Samuel Johnson was at a gathering one evening when a young man essayed a bassoon solo. Johnson visibly winced, and his neighbor whispered reassuringly, "You know, Doctor, that the bassoon is very difficult to play."

"You may well say so, sir," said Johnson. "And I only wish to God it were impossible!"

Two of our greatest popular composers, Richard Rodgers and the late Cole Porter, were alike inasmuch as they worked fast and without temperament. Once when a friend asked Rodgers' partner, Oscar Hammerstein, what it was like to work with Rodgers, he said, "I just hand him a lyric and jump out of the way."

And when a reporter asked Cole Porter what his greatest source of inspiration was, he replied, "A telephone call from a producer."

Austrian-born conductor Hans Richter, leading the Duesseldorf Orchestra in a concert, became painfully aware of a man in the front row rhythmically tapping his foot. Richter contained his annoyance during the allegro, but suddenly became "scherzo-phrenic" in the andante. He stopped the orchestra, wheeled around and, gazing gimlet-eyed at the offender, said with smoldering sarcasm, "I'm sorry to trouble you, but I cannot always keep time with your foot."

Shortly after Charles Gounod died, in 1893, a second-rate German composer called on Johannes Brahms and proudly showed him the score of his latest work. "It is a funeral march in honor of our dear friend Gounod," he explained. "What do you think of it?"

The testy Brahms looked it over through the smoke of his ever-present cigar. Finally he handed it back and said, "It would have been better if you had died and Gounod had written the march."

Jack Benny likes to credit his father with a gem of musical criticism. Back in Waukegan, Jack practiced faithfully on his violin each day. One Saturday a neighboring dog passed by and started howling dolefully under the window of the room where Jack was sawing away. Finally his father shouted downstairs, "For pity's sake, Jack, can't you play some piece the dog doesn't know!"

Which reminds me of the pithy way Fred Allen once described the noises emanating from Jack's violin: "It sounds like the strings are back in the cat."

Mrs. Cornelius Vanderbilt, fabulously wealthy arbiter of New York's social *crème de la crème*, once asked violin virtuoso Fritz Kreisler how much he would charge to play a short recital at a very posh affair she was planning in her palatial home.

"My fee is eighteen thousand dollars," said Mr. Kreisler.

"That's agreeable," replied Mrs. Vanderbilt. "But I hope you understand that you should not mingle with my guests."

"Oh! Well, in that case, my fee is only five hundred dollars," said Mr. Kreisler.

Sam Goldwyn, king of the accidental ad-lib, was at a big dinner party and was introduced to the French sculptor Giacometti. "Say, you're just the one who could give me some good advice," said Sam. "Have you met my wife, Frances?"

"Yes, just a moment ago," said Giacometti. "She is very beautiful."

"Did you notice her hands?"

"Yes, as a matter of fact, I did. They are very lovely."

"Well, here's my idea. I want to get a bust made of them."

The late Albert Einstein was an amateur violinist. Once at Princeton, he was visited by Jascha Heifetz, Gregor Piatigorsky, and Artur Rubinstein.

They suggested that Einstein join them in a little chamber music. He jumped at the opportunity and quickly produced his violin to join the group in a delicate Mozart quartet.

After a few moments, Rubinstein looked up in annoyance. "My dear Dr. Einstein," he protested, "what's wrong with you? Can't you count?"

Humorist Don Herold, completely bald and unheroic-looking, was asked by his friend Sigmund Spaeth how he liked opera. "Well, let's put it this way," said Don, "I'd rather sing it than listen to it."

In this, he echoed the opinion of Mayor Jimmy Walker concerning opera: "If you get there before it's finished, you're on time."

But they were both beaten to the punch by Mark Twain, who said after a performance of *Tannhäuser* in Vienna, "Wagner's music isn't as bad as it sounds."

Madame Schumann-Heink—all three hundred splendid pounds of her—was trying to make an entrance onto a concert stage in Baltimore, but the musicians were so crowded together that she became entangled with fiddle bows and music stands. One of the violinists said out of the corner of his mouth, "Try walking sideways!"

Madame hissed, "Sidevays—mein Gott, I haff no sidevays!"

Critics on the Hearth

CRITICS abound in every walk of life, as you will see by this section. Of course, theater critics, who are *paid* to make nasty remarks, have the best fun. But even amateur theater critics make out pretty well. Playwright George Kaufman, after viewing a play called *The Ladder,* gave his immortal opinion: "I saw it under adverse conditions—the curtain was up."

My own favorite is a remark by veteran newspaperman Bide Dudley about a long-forgotten play: "It was so terrible that the audience even hissed the ushers."

Hobe Morrison, *Variety's* great historian of the legitimate theater, once attended the out-of-town opening of a play called *Hollywood Be Thy Name.* Early in the first act, it became apparent that the show was a total turkey—witless and jumbled. Chaos came to a climax when one character pointed a gun at another and fired—without sound. The actor clicked the gun a second time while his victim waited hopefully to drop dead—but still no sound. There was a third, then a fourth click of the gun, but still no surcease from agony. Finally the desperate stage manager dropped the curtain.

Immediately after, there was a sharp gun report from the stage. Hobe Morrison rose from his seat and sighed, "Well, at least he got the author!"

Dustin Farnum, a minor theatrical genius, was once expounding upon his triumphs to Oliver Herford. "This play I'm in at present," he said, "really shows me off to best advantage. Last night I had the audience glued to their seats."

"Ingenious," said Herford. "How clever of you to have thought of it!"

Which is rather like another item about a second-rate Shakespearian who went about London telling all his acquaintances, "Next Monday I am opening at the Haymarket Theater in *Macbeth*." When he finally encountered James M. Barrie and apprised him of the good news, Barrie said, "Thanks for the warning."

Robert Benchley usually wrote down his "ad-libs" in reviews and articles. But there is a real ad-lib on record that occurred while he was drama critic for the old *Life* magazine. He attended the first night of a horrendous South Seas melodrama called *The Squall*. It was famous only for a scantily clad native beauty who was determined to break up the marriage of a white couple on the island. She kept saying to the wife (played by Blanche Yurka, no less), "Me Nubi. Nubi help you in house. Nubi good girl. Nubi stay?"

Along about the middle of the second act, Benchley could stand it no longer. After the fifth "Me Nubi. Nubi good girl. Nubi stay?" he rose and whispered to neighboring playgoers, "Me Bobbie. Bobbie bad boy. Bobbie go!"

A fifth-rate playwright, whose talent fell several notches short of his bloated image of himself, had been pestering the life out of showman Charles Frohman to get a play produced—but without success.

"Isn't there any way we can get this play onstage?" he pleaded after being turned down for the seventh time by the venerable showman.

"Well, there is one way," replied Frohman. "We can grind it up and use it as a snowstorm."

There is an old story about the English professor whose wife caught him kissing the maid. "Henry, I am surprised!" she said. "No, my dear," he replied. "It is I who am surprised—you are amazed."

The joke probably is a "switch" on a famous remark of Dr. Samuel Johnson, father of the English dictionary. Dr. Johnson, as slovenly as he was brilliant, attended a dinner party one evening, and the lady next to him could stand his proximity no longer. "Dr. Johnson," she said, "you smell."

To which the good Doctor rumbled, "Madam, you should learn to be more precise: You *smell*—I *stink*."

A grave literary reporter once asked the five-foot-two Truman Capote, "Very seriously, Mr. Capote, how would *you* describe yourself?"

Capote thought for a moment and said, "Well, I'm about as tall as a shotgun and just as noisy."

Look editor Myrick ("Mike") Land turned up a fine Gertrude Stein ad-lib in his book *The Fine Art of Literary Mayhem*. The running feud between Miss Stein and Ernest Hemingway lasted for years. Hemingway gained a point when he had a character in *For Whom the Bell Tolls* paraphrase the famed Stein line: "A rose is a rose is a rose." Said the character, "An onion is an onion is an onion. A stone is a Stein is a rock is a pebble."

Gertrude managed to top that one afternoon at a literary gathering on the Left Bank. A reporter asked her if she believed in the old story that if a million monkeys were given a million typewriters, they could quite by chance turn out a classic like *Macbeth*.

"Quite possible," she said. "I'm told that they've already finished a novel called *For Whom the Bell Tolls*."

George M. Cohan always had a soft spot in his heart for one particular drama critic, who showed more imagination than most in the novel way he attacked a certain play. The first-night performance, which the critic was attending, got off on a bad foot and never righted itself. During the first act, a trickle of disappointed first-nighters began walking out. Between the acts more left. At the end of the second, a wild-eyed multitude began rushing for the exits. At this moment the critic arose from his seat towards the rear of the theater and held up his arms in a restraining gesture. "Stop!" he shouted in his best shipwreck voice. "Women and children first!"

A sort of counter-ad-lib occurred when Arthur Godfrey received a missive from a lady fan. She wrote, "This is only a suggestion, but I think that more people would believe that your program is ad-lib if you'd stop rattling your ad-libs near the microphone."

Director Billy Wilder's very life is a series of ad-libs, but he probably topped himself on his return from making a picture in Paris. When newsmen asked what he thought of France, he said, "Well, I'll tell you—it's the kind of a place where the money falls apart in your hands and you can't tear the toilet paper."

Clarence Darrow was a sharp wit both in and out of court. When Calvin Coolidge was running for President in 1924, a reporter asked Darrow what he thought of Cal's qualifications. "Coolidge," he said, "is the greatest man ever to come out of Plymouth, Vermont."

But perhaps Darrow's greatest ad-lib came during an important trial, when his rage against injustice mounted to such fury that he refused point-blank to answer a question from the bench.

"Mr. Darrow," snapped the judge, "are you trying to show contempt for this court?"

"No, sir," rumbled Darrow. "I'm trying to conceal it!"

Millionaire Harry Thaw shot architect Sanford White in a quarrel over the lovely Evelyn Nesbitt (1917). Thaw was given ten years in Sing Sing Prison. Shortly after he was released, he attended the grand opening of the Roxy Theater in New York. As he gazed in horror at the Hollywood-Byzantine splendor of the lobby, he gasped, "My God, I shot the wrong architect!"

Sir Thomas Beecham was conducting the triumphal scene of Verdi's *Aida* at Covent Garden when one of the horses committed a grievous social error. Beecham turned to the audience and said, "A distressing spectacle, ladies and gentlemen, but gad, what a critic!"

Booze,
Beefsteak, and Belly Laughs

MAN's mellowest comments on life are ofttimes distilled after he has "fed the inner man" or "slipped out of a wet bathing suit and into a dry martini." (Incidentally, that ad-lib is almost always attributed to Bob Benchley, but his son Nat tells me that Benchley never said it. So it was probably Alexander Woollcott.)

Anyway, good grog, good grub, and good gags will always go together, at least until the morning after.

For six months author Don Marquis had stuck faithfully to his vow to give up liquor. One night he strolled up to the bar at the Players Club and stunned the bartender by ordering a double Scotch, explaining, "I'm trying to lick this damn will power of mine."

John Barrymore, the "great profile," had ordered lobster at Shanley's, the gastronomical gathering place for theatrical figures of the early 1900's. Jack complained imperiously to the waiter that one of his lobster's claws was missing.

"They fight in the kitchen, and sometimes bite each other's claws off," apologized the waiter.

"Then take this crustacean back and bring me the winner," said Barrymore.

Frank Case, the kindly literary-minded proprietor of the Algonquin Hotel, was worried about tenant John Barrymore's over-drinking habits. Hearing Barrymore order an absinthe frappé for breakfast one morning, Case sought to distract him from alcohol by inviting him to have coffee. Barrymore savored three cups and by the time his absinthe arrived no longer hankered for it. Next day Barrymore met his friend Case in the lobby.

"That's a great idea of yours, Frank—really wonderful."

"What's so wonderful?" queried Case.

"Coffee for breakfast," said Barrymore.

The late Sherman Billingsley was appalled one night to see an out-of-towner at a Stork Club table dining country-bumpkin style with a napkin tucked under his chin. Beckoning discreetly to a waiter, the dignified club owner whispered, "Tell that man we don't do that here—but don't hurt his feelings."

The waiter dutifully sauntered over to the napkin-gusseted patron and asked solicitously, "Shave or a haircut, sir?"

A famous liquor ad-lib has been credited to just about every tippler imaginable—from General Grant through Bob Benchley to Dean Martin—but I have pretty good authority that it originated with W. C. Fields. Fields, playing in the old *Ziegfeld Follies,* had a trunkful of gin bottles in his dressing room. One evening Flo Ziegfeld, a fretful man, watched Fields start on his fifth martini and groaned, "Will, you really should stay off those things—they're slow death!"

Rasped Fields, "Don't worry, sire—I'm in no hurry."

It was Fields, too, who attended a cocktail party during Prohibition and disdainfully turned down an "orange blossom" cocktail, which he felt was an insult to honest gin.

"But, Will," said his host, "this gin was made from U.S. grain alcohol."

"I don't doubt it," said Fields, "but there's been a lot of bad oranges going around."

Samuel Johnson attended a dinner given by a hostess noted for the small portions she served her guests. The meager forkfuls did little more than whet the great lexicographer's voracious appetite. At the end of the dinner, as Johnson sipped disconsolately at a thimbleful of coffee, the society dowager chirped, "Now do tell me, Dr. Johnson, when we may expect the pleasure of having you dine with us again?"

"Immediately, madam; immediately."

During an election campaign, Abe Lincoln stopped off for lunch at a rural inn in Ohio, where the cuisine was primitive at best. The waiter served him a hot drink in a cup, and Abe took one taste.

"Waiter," he said gently, "if this is coffee, please bring me some tea. If this is tea, please bring me some coffee."

Jack Carter tells about the night he was in Prince Mike Romanoff's plush Hollywood restaurant when a well-known movie juvenile came in with a buxom wench swathed in a long mink coat. The lady was well oiled and, after a few uninhibited dance steps, it became obvious to all that she was stark-naked under the mink coat.

The dignified Prince Mike rushed to the actor and whispered wildly, "My God, dear boy, you'll take her out of here quickly, won't you?"

"You bet," said the actor. "Did you think I was going to leave her here for you?"

Painter James Whistler once entered the dining room of a London club and stopped by the table of a friend who had a plate of unsavory-looking stew before him. Whistler gasped, "Gad, old chap, are you going to eat that—or *have* you?"

Director Lewis Milestone was making a picture called *The Captain Hates the Sea*, with a cast of all-star drunks.

Production of the film grew slower. Skies were overcast and Milestone maneuvered the ship about the Southern California waters in search of sun. Often he found some, only to discover the wind too fierce or the actors too drunk for the dialogue to be clear.

Exposed film dribbled into the studio, and the studio head was fuming. In desperation he fired off a cable to Milestone: "Hurry up. The cost is staggering."

Milestone cabled back: "So is the cast."

An ad-lib that is prepared in advance is not a true ad-lib by any means. But I can't resist reporting one that concerned a certain Hollywood character actress named Gisella Werbezirk-von Piffl, which happens to be an aristocratic name in Austria.

In any case, a Hollywood wag with an extra martini under his belt once called her on the phone: "Hello, is this Gisella Werbezirk-von Piffl?"

"Yes," she replied very correctly.

"Did you, by any chance, attend P.S. 38 with me in New York City?"

"No, it is not possible."

"Oh, I'm sorry," said the wag. "I must have gotten the wrong Gisella Werbezirk-von Piffl."

In London during the austere V-2 days, the future Governor of California, Ronald Reagan, was surprised to find pheasant on the Savoy Hotel menu. Unfortunately the hotel's pheasant plucker had gone to war, and the fowl was served with its feathers and yellow legs still intact. Said actor Mike O'Shea with whom Reagan was dining, "Waiter, bring me some liniment. I'll have this bird flying again in ten minutes."

The Social Security Set

THERE IS something especially reassuring about the humor of "senior citizens" (what a dismal expression!). Maybe it's because we all know that we'll finally head for the same port. In this department, there is no question about the perfect gem. It is practically a trademark of the rosy-cheeked septuagenarian Maurice Chevalier. When asked by a reporter if he minded being so old, he said, "Oh, it's not so bad—when you consider the alternative."

There is another classic that I'm very fond of. It has been attributed to many oldsters, but I think the great British comedian A. E. Matthews coined it. "Matty," as he was known all over the world, was asked, on his eightieth birthday, what his daily routine was.

"Well," he said, "I wake up and ring my butler for the London *Times*. Then I look at the obituary page, and if my name's not on it, I get up."

At a White House news conference in 1960, a reporter asked President Eisenhower, "Sir, do you realize that on your upcoming birthday you will be the oldest President ever to serve?"

Ike smiled wryly. "I believe," he said, "it's a tradition in baseball that when a pitcher has a no-hitter going for him, nobody reminds him of it."

Even in his last years, Winston Churchill liked to drop in at the House of Commons from time to time. One day when he was helped down the aisle to his seat by two aides, a couple of young M.P.'s nearby started murmuring about the spectacle. "You know, I really don't think he should come in any more," said one. "He's getting so tottery."

The other whispered, "Yes, and they say he's even getting a bit soft in the upper story."

Churchill slowly turned in his seat and rasped, "They also say that he's getting hard-of-hearing."

One night in the Lambs Club bar, David Wayne told a risqué story that drew a laugh from everybody but eighty-year-old Harry Hershfield. Wayne said, "What's the matter, Harry—can't you remember when you went out with girls?"

Said veteran Hershfield, "Sure, I can remember when I went out with girls—but I can't remember what for."

Harry made his first trip to Paris when he was rather well on in years. He told a friend he wished he'd seen it forty years ago.

"You mean when Paris was really Paris?" queried his friend.

"No," said Harry, "when Hershfield was really Hershfield."

For many years Hershfield had always phoned Bernard Baruch on his birthday no matter where he was in the world . . . Europe, Israel . . . to wish him well.

On Baruch's ninety-fifth birthday, Hershfield phoned him. During the course of the conversation, he asked, "Bernie, do you think there's as much love in the world today as there was years back?"

"Yes," was the reply, "but there's another bunch doing it!"

70

When Baruch was asked about a certain very boring Wall Street tycoon, he chuckled: "I have not had my hearing aid open to that man for years."

Bob Hope and Bing Crosby were taking it easy between shootings on one of their many *Road to Zanzibar* pictures. Hope mentioned that he'd heard Frank Sinatra a few nights before. (This was when Sinatra was not as famous as he is today.) "Bing," he said, "I'm convinced that this kid Sinatra is a singer who comes along once in a lifetime."

"Yeah," said Bing. "But why did he have to come along in *my* lifetime!"

The frisky Mary Garden was seated opposite the noted industrialist, politician, and after-dinner speaker Chauncey Depew at a banquet. Throughout dinner he kept staring down her low-necked dress until finally she asked what was so hypnotizing. He replied, "I wonder, Miss Garden, what keeps that gown on you?"

"Only your extreme old age, Mr. Depew," answered Miss Garden.

When Pablo Casals gave his famous concert at the White House, a reporter asked, during a press conference, "Sir, I understand you still practice at least six hours a day. Why do you feel that is necessary at this stage in your career?"

"Because," said Casals, "I think I'm beginning to make some progress."

Old Curmudgeon Harold Ickes, Secretary of the Interior under FDR, was waylaid in the lobby of the Mayflower Hotel by a rich old biddy whom he had met at some cocktail party to which his wife had bodily dragged him. "And

how do you find yourself these brisk winter mornings?"
prattled the Mayflower matron.

To which Mr. Ickes growled, "I just throw back the
comforter, madam, and there I am!"

Ickes made a searing political ad-lib some years ago,
when an aide told him that Thomas Dewey had announced
his intention to seek the Republican nomination for President.

"Ah, so," said Mr. Ickes. "Dewey has tossed his diaper
into the ring."

Getting There
Is Half the Fun

THERE IS something about an elevator that generates a surprising number of ad-libs. In fact, any kind of public conveyance seems to inspire wits—maybe because there is a more or less captive audience available.

What must be the grandfather of all elevator jokes was told me by Dick Dodson, an old-time editor. He was a messenger at Harper's when Mark Twain was the firm's star author. Once he was awe-struck at meeting the great man in the elevator. Twain, resplendent in his customary white suit, puffing a large cigar, patted the young fellow on the shoulder and said, "Work hard, young fellow, and invest your money wisely. Someday you'll be smoking dollar cigars like me."

Young Dodson, wide-eyed, gasped, "Are they *really* dollar cigars, sir?"

"Yup," said Mark ("Ham") Twain. "Dollar a barrel."

"Fat" Jack Leonard is one of those comedians who is always "on." A few years back, when compact taxis were new in New York, Jack and his manager emerged from Lindy's Restaurant and hailed a cab. After Jack had huffed and puffed his way through the door, the driver asked, "Where to?"

Said Jack, "Drive me to a bigger cab."

The streets were wet, the martinis were dry, and when humorist Robert Benchley emerged from an elegant New York night club, he asked the resplendently uniformed man at the door to call him a taxi.

"Sir, I happen to be an Admiral of the Fleet in the United States Navy," snorted the affronted gent.

"Very well, then," said Benchley, "call me a battleship!"

The great Negro educator Booker T. Washington received a telegram asking if he could address an important meeting of college presidents. Time was short. He packed feverishly and hurried to the nearest hack stand. "I'm in a great hurry," he told the cabdriver. "Can you drive me to the railway station?"

The cabbie spat a bit of tobacco juice and said, "I ain't never driven this horse for a black man and I never will."

"That's all right," said Washington. "Jump into the back seat and I'll drive you."

It worked—he caught his train.

Recently Milton Berle landed at Los Angeles airport and went to rent a car at the desk of the company that "tries harder." Berle was wearing his usual dark glasses, and the Avis girl peered at him. "Aren't you Phil Silvers?"

"That," snorted Berle, "is why you are 'Number Two.'"

Fred Allen's barbs have been repeated so often that I can't understand why this one is not better known:

One night Fred went to see a preview of a movie at one of those small projection rooms in the producing company's office building. As usual, after the showing everyone tried to crush into the single elevator on duty. Fred found himself wedged in next to a plump lady who began to get hysterical as the operator tried to shut the door. "My hus-

band's left behind!" she cried. "You can't go without my husband!"

"Courage, madam," said Fred. "This elevator may be going down, but it's not the *Titanic*."

The indestructible British comedienne Margaret Rutherford came to New York a few years back to do a play and treat herself to a round of shopping. Her old friend Melville Cooper had just undergone a tonsillectomy, so she went up to Presbyterian Hospital to pay him a visit. Poor Miss Rutherford was awed by the great building, particularly since she'd never been "in hospital" herself. When the elevator man asked her which floor she wished, she became confused.

"Dear me; oh, dear me," she bumbled, and then brightened. "Gentlemen's Tonsils, please."

One of Bennett Cerf's favorite ad-libs has nothing to do with the theater or publishing. He tells it about his neighbor in Mt. Kisco: Mr. Albritson looks like a typical, docile commuter, but he has a cutting wit. One morning, in the non-smoking car of a local train, a loud-mouthed type squeezed his fat self in beside Mr. Albritson, lit up a cigar, and said, "My smoking won't bother you, will it, friend?"

Mr. Albritson replied, "Not at all—so long as my getting sick won't bother *you*."

The English statesman Lord Rosebery was famed for his cool, immediate solutions to every possible diplomatic problem. Once he was crossing the Channel with his beloved collie dog. A stiff wave caught the dog off balance, and over the side he went.

"Stop the ship, Captain!" shouted Rosebery. "My dog is overboard!"

"I'm so sorry, your Lordship," said the captain, "but my orders allow me to stop the ship only for a human being."

"I quite understand your predicament," said Rosebery, "but I believe it can be circumvented." Whereupon he dove overboard.

The great Cunarder *Queen Mary* has gone to rest, bless her soul, but not without leaving some fine ad-libs in her wake. My favorite goes back to another noble British lady, Bea Lillie. Bea shipped aboard the *Mary* on her first return trip to England. She surveyed the vastness of the liner with wide-open eyes and pursed lips. "Goodness," she murmured, "what time does this place get to England?"

Some attribute this story to Mamie Van Doren, but a little sleuthing on my part reveals it was Monique Van Vooren. It seems that Monique, the very brainy (I.Q. 156) Belgian beauty, was driving home in heavy traffic one evening when her motor suddenly went dead and her car blocked traffic for miles behind. While other drivers ungallantly honked their horns in a maddening din, Mlle. Van Vooren climbed imperturbably from her stalled car, slammed the door, shuffled up to the klaxon-clown in the car right behind her, and said, "I'll be glad to sit here and toot your horn for you if you'll try to get my car started."

Joe Frisco, the stuttering comedian, was walking one day on Hollywood Boulevard and imprudently started to cross the street against a red light. A policeman caught up with him and snapped, "I've got to give you a ticket."

Joe asked, "How f-f-fast was I going, officer?"

Groucho Marx, the grand-dad-libber of modern times, was traveling by air and requested permission to smoke a cigar. There's a fairly hard-and-fast regulation on commercial airlines against this particular aromatic indulgence. But the hostess felt that perhaps in the case of a passenger as famous as Groucho Marx the rules might be relaxed.

"I suppose you can smoke a cigar if you don't annoy the lady passengers," she said.

To which Groucho quickly replied, "You mean I've got a choice?"

Dames A-Dueling

POSSIBLY because women have one more rib than men, they are particularly adept at ad-ribbing. They do very well when pitted against the male, but are at their best in female combat.

Dorothy Parker, of course, is their standard-bearer, and her most classic of many classics is a relatively fond remark to a young wife who had become quite large in the last months of pregnancy. In fact she kept her friends nervous by insisting on attending plays right up till the last moment. When that moment finally arrived, and she was successfully delivered of a child, Dorothy said, "Congratulations, my dear—we all knew you had it in you!"

A gaggle of Hollywood actresses was gathered at Rosalind Russell's house discussing that old black female bugaboo—age. One of the "girls" got a faraway look in her eyes and said, "I dread the thought of forty-five."

"Why? What happened to you then, dear?" cooed Miss Russell demurely.

Beatrice Lillie, perhaps the most amiable and unassuming noble lady of our time, has one point of vanity—a fabulous string of pearls that she inherited by virtue of her marriage to the late Sir Robert Peel. One evening at a swank London party, Bea was wearing the "Peel pearls," and a shrewish dowager approached to inspect them. "Miss

Lillie," she said, "I have been told that a sure way to tell whether pearls are real is to bite them."

"Bite away," said Bea. "But mind you, it only works if your teeth are real."

Bea almost never refers to her true title, which is Lady Peel. But one night she was invited with some other stars to a huge supper party given by a New Jersey frankfurter king. After a veritable swimming-pool of champagne had been consumed, the guests started to leave. Bea overheard her socially ambitious hostess murmur to a couple, "I hope you don't feel that there were too many theatrical persons here." Whereupon she advanced on the firmly gusseted lady and announced in loud tones, "Alas, it has come time for Lady Peel to bid good night to the butcher's wife."

Hermione Gingold was a guest on a TV show, and the M.C. asked if she knew Phyllis Diller. He might have expected a slightly cool answer, since lady comedians are apt to be a bit competitive. Hermione said, "I have met Miss Diller."

The M.C. persisted: "And what do you think of her?"

Hermione smiled tautly. "Oh, just another pretty face."

Bette Davis is a pretty spry innuendo-caster when she gets started. One evening at The Colony restaurant, she was dining with several friends when a bespangled starlet of no uncertain virtue passed the table and cooed, "Hello, Bette—so nice to see you."

A naïve chap at the table asked Miss Davis, "Who *is* that fascinating girl that just passed by?"

"That, darling," said Miss Davis, "is the original good time that was had by all."

The Paris salons of the "Belle Epoque" were famous as hotbeds of scandalous gossip. One evening Mme. Baignières, a young woman both pretty and witty, arrived late and found a group of ladies in heated discussion. "Ah, Madame," said her hostess, "you are just in time to give us your views on a fascinating subject—adultery."

"Oh, dear!" said Mme. Baignières. "I must have confused the dates—I came prepared on incest."

When Carol Channing was trouping *Hello, Dolly!* on the West Coast, there was the inevitable cocktail party for the press in each city. Carol is the reporters' darling—they know they can ask her almost anything and get a bubbling answer. That is, *almost* anything. At one party, a lady reporter chirped up, "Miss Channing, do you remember the most embarrassing moment of your life?"

"Yes, I certainly do," said Carol. "Next question?"

The late Elsa Maxwell, social arbitress and party-arranger for the elite, spied a gate-crasher at a big affair she had planned for a New York debutante. Approaching the intruder as he savored a caviar-laden cracker, she held out her hand à la gracious hostess and beamed: "I heard you were looking for me—because you wanted to say good night."

The stars often find themselves on the wrong end of ad-libs when they run up against their loving public. Imogene Coca likes to tell of the time that a Helen Hokinson-type lady approached her in the lobby of the Plaza and said, "I'm *sure* I remember you from the Sid Caesar Show . . . Didn't you used to be Imogene Coca?"

Novelist Mary McCarthy once lectured at a swank ladies' club in Boston and was fascinated by the style of hats that the membership sported: such discreet items as passenger-pigeon plumes and Ming Dynasty velvet.

During lunch, she asked a Mrs. Peabody: "Tell me, my dear, where do you Boston ladies get your hats?"

Mrs. Peabody drew herself up. "Miss McCarthy, we do not *get* our hats—we *have* our hats."

Which reminds me of the last time I myself was in Boston and noticed a terribly literary ad-lib from the Fire Department in the Ritz Hotel. (Maybe it's not a true ad-lib, but it's the closest that any fire department will ever make.) Over the revolving door of the Ritz is a large sign implying that the Boston Fire Department does not approve of revolving doors. It warns: THIS IS NOT AN ACCREDITED EGRESS!

Alexander Woollcott was almost as famous for the insults he received as for the insults he gave. One day at the "Round Table" in the Algonquin Hotel, he was leading a discussion about producing an all-star revival of *Macbeth,* when actress Peggy Wood arrived.

"Now, here's a good point," said Woollcott. "Peggy would *not* make a good Lady Macbeth, would she?"

Miss Wood looked the pudgy crosspatch straight in the eye: "No, Aleck, but *you* would."

But Aleck got in his licks too. Harpo Marx once arrived to spend a weekend at Woollcott's famous summer home in Vermont. Harpo had borrowed from Ben Hecht a wreck of a car which just about suited the Marx personality.

"What's *that* thing?" asked Woollcott.

"That's my town car," said Harpo defensively.

"What town—Pompeii?"

Columnist Earl Wilson once asked the whiskey-tenor, Tallulah Bankhead, "Have you ever been mistaken for a man?"

"No, dahling. Have you?"

Dorothy Parker was at a dinner party one evening when the subject of Clare Booth Luce came up. Between heated peaks in the ensuing argument, a lady guest remarked, "Well, you must admit that Clare is always very considerate toward her inferiors."

Miss Parker murmured, "Where does she find them?"

One of the less well-known Dorothy Parker ad-libs occurred at an after-theater party given by Jules Brulatour, a rich businessman. As Miss Parker was about to make her way into the powder room, she nearly collided with a catty young actress who was not universally beloved. The actress dramatically deferred to Miss Parker, saying, "Age before beauty."

Miss Parker stepped through the door ahead of the lass, turned her head, and said with a smile, "And pearls before swine."

Washington Confidential

FROM Ptolemy to Pericles and Disraeli to Dirksen, law-making and phrase-making have gone hand-in-hand—sometimes foot-in-mouth. Down in Washington, D.C., there are many who feel that the *Congressional Record* is the funniest book ever compiled. So here are my favorites from the town that George Washington, Abraham Lincoln, and Millard Fillmore made famous.

And there is one classic that I cannot ignore, though it is well known to millions, because it will probably be quoted by our great-grandchildren: When a little boy asked President Kennedy, "Mr. President, how did you become a war hero?" J.F.K. replied, "It was absolutely involuntary—they sank my boat."

Adlai Stevenson told a story about his fellow Princetonian Woodrow Wilson. When he was Governor of New Jersey, he received a call from Washington advising him that his good friend, a United States Senator from New Jersey, had just died. Wilson was so shocked he immediately canceled all appointments and sat at his desk stunned. Within a few minutes of receiving the bad news he had a phone call from a New Jersey politician who said bluntly, "Governor, I would like to take the Senator's place."

Wilson said nothing for a moment, and then replied, "Well, you may quote me as saying that's perfectly agreeable to me if it's agreeable to the undertaker."

When Harry Truman was vacating the White House in 1953, he sank exhausted into a chair and stared glumly at the huge piles of crates: "If I'd known how much packing I'd have to do, I'd have run for another term!"

President Taft had to take a good deal of joshing because of his tremendous girth. One day he was visiting Theodore Roosevelt at his seaside home in Oyster Bay, and decided to take a dip in the surf. One of the Roosevelt children bounded into the house from a game of croquet and chirped, "Daddy, may we take a swim?"

"Not just now, dear," said Roosevelt. "The President is using the ocean."

But Mr. Taft had his wits about him too. Once when he was giving a campaign speech in a rural district, a dissident yokel tossed a cabbage onto the platform. Taft gave the cabbage a sidelong glance and said, "It appears that one of my opponents has lost his head."

Oscar Levant and wife Joan were among a group of show-business guests at a White House dinner during the Truman administration. It was one of those half-social, half-command performance soirées and, after cordials, Oscar obliged with a twenty-minute piano recital. After shaking hands with the President and while waiting for his rented limousine to whisk them away from the White House portico, Oscar was overheard grumbling to his wife, "Now I guess we owe the Trumans a dinner."

Carl T. Rowan, the Negro journalist who has been head of USIA and former Ambassador to Finland, was mowing the lawn one afternoon at his comfortable home in a substantial Washington neighborhood. A large sports car pulled up at the curb and the loud-voiced-type driver yelled, "Hey, boy, how much do you charge for a lawn like that?"

Rowan hesitated, then smiled. "Nothing," he said. "The lady of the house lets me live with her."

Calvin Coolidge, as parsimonious with his words as with his governmental expenditures, was a past master at finding excuses for not speaking. At one whistle stop during his campaign for election he appeared on the observation platform, sized up the crowd, and ducked back into his private car. "This crowd," he said, "is too big for an anecdote and too small for an oration."

Charles G. ("Hell-and-Maria") Dawes once did a stint as Ambassador to Great Britain. Upon returning home, he gave a speech in which he said, "American diplomacy is easy on the brain but hell on the feet."

Henry P. Fletcher, himself a career diplomat, turned to his neighbor and murmured, "It depends on which you use."

In 1959, when the U. S. Post Office, deeply embroiled in censorship, refused to deliver certain books and magazines, a great many people felt that censorship was the business of legal courts, not the Post Office.

Senator Gale McGee, when asked by a reporter what his plans were for the upcoming session of Congress, said, "I'm going to introduce a resolution to have the Postmaster General stop reading dirty books and deliver the mail."

Edward Everett Hale, when he was Chaplain of the Senate, made light of both religion and politics. Asked, "Do you pray for the Senators, Mr. Hale?" he answered, "No, I look at the Senators and pray for the country."

Low Humor in High Places

ROYALTY and heads of state have a running head start when it comes to ad-libs. Almost *anything* faintly humorous that they say is scribbled down by a hundred reporters. Perhaps this is the basis of fame for Prince Philip of England's reply to a question, "What would be your advice as to how one should conduct oneself during a royal celebration?"

Said the Prince, "Always seize any opportunity to go to the toilet."

In a much sweeter vein, I shall always love Victoria's reaction to a humble ad-lib during her Golden Jubilee Celebration. When she returned to the palace after the parade, a lady-in-waiting asked what she liked best about the day. Victoria thought and said, "I think it was a rough-looking fellow who managed to stick his head in my carriage."

"Good heavens!" gasped the lady-in-waiting. "What did he say?"

Victoria smiled. "He said, '*Go* it, old girl!'"

Prime Minister Macmillan has been both the author and the butt of a good deal of political wit and invective. Perhaps the best-known example of his wit occurred when his speech before the United Nations in New York, on September 29, 1960, was interrupted by the Russian Premier, Khrushchev, who took off his shoe and pounded on the table with it. In the best tradition of British unflappability, Macmillan remarked calmly, "I'd like to have that translated, if I may."

During the grandiose Jubilee Celebration of Queen Victoria's fiftieth year on the British throne, Queen Liliuokalani of the Hawaiian Islands paid a courtesy call on the great monarch at Windsor Castle. In their get-acquainted chat, the Hawaiian queen revealed that she had English blood in her veins.

"How can that be?" asked Victoria.

"One of my ancestors ate Captain Cook," replied Liliuokalani.

In 1955, Lyndon Johnson ordered two suits from a swank Washington tailor. Shortly afterwards Johnson suffered a serious heart attack. The tailor called an aide at the hospital and asked if he should proceed with the order.

Johnson told the aide, "Tell him to go ahead with the dark-blue suit—we can use that no matter what happens."

Premier Georges Clemenceau, the great "Tiger of France," managed to turn the tide of the First World War almost single-handedly. One day at a meeting with his ministers, Clemenceau made an important decision that astounded many of the group. "But Monsieur le Premier," said one, "this is not in agreement with the thinking of the General Staff."

Clemenceau rumbled, "War is too serious an affair to leave to generals."

At the dinner table one evening Lord Chesterfield chided his butler because the dinner plates were not clean.

"But, milord," alibied the servant, "they say that everyone eats a peck of dirt in his lifetime anyway."

"Perhaps," replied Chesterfield, "but not all at one meal."

The great French diplomat Talleyrand was driving in the Bois de Boulogne with a boring German statesman who persisted in discussing the technicalities of a certain treaty. Talleyrand noticed that a passenger in the carriage drawing alongside was delivering himself of a tremendous yawn. He nudged the German statesman and whispered, "Shh! I fear that you are overheard!"

The most glamorous of all Parisian courtesans was "La Belle Otéro," who consoled many a prince and millionaire. The lady considered herself the Queen of Paris and conducted herself accordingly. One night she went to the Comédie Française and draped herself in her favorite box. The manager bustled up and said, "Madame, tonight this box has been reserved for others."

"Let them sit elsewhere," she commanded.

"But it is impossible this time," moaned the manager. "It is the Czar of Russia and his party. You must leave."

"Very well," she snapped. And as she swept by the waiting Czar, she said, "Sir, never again will I serve my guests caviar!"

King Frederick of Denmark is quite proud of his impeccable English, and therefore was no doubt especially pleased when an American TV network asked to shoot some documentary scenes of the royal household. One of the photographic team was a stunning young blonde, and while she was helping to set up a shot of His Highness on the throne, the blonde tripped over a lighting cable and landed at his feet in a provocative display of nylon and lace. King Frederick did not move a single muscle of his face. His aspect was one-hundred-per-cent grave and noble, but he murmured out of the corner of his mouth to the TV commentator, "Wasn't that a dainty dish to set before the King!"

Strange as it may seem, women drivers posed a traffic problem in the narrow, twisted streets of Paris even in the pre-revolutionary days of King Louis XVI. It was the custom for society ladies of the time to chauffeur their own carriages, and not even the King dared risk their displeasure by forbidding them to drive. Summoning one of his sharpest troubleshooters, Count d'Argenson, the King asked him whether he could diplomatically unsnarl the traffic jams.

"Mais bien entendu, mon sire," said d'Argenson. "I will simply promulgate a law: 'Ladies under thirty years of age are forbidden to drive carriages.' "

Whatever your political feelings may be about President de Gaulle, you must admit that he has sharp flashes of wit. One of his aides, Constantin Melnick, tells of a moment when "le grand Charles" was having more than ordinary difficulty in conciliating France's numerous political parties. He raised his hands and cried, "*Mon Dieu,* how can you be expected to govern a country that has two hundred and forty-six kinds of cheese!"

And at an important reception, when the speaker introduced him as a modern Robespierre, he remarked, "I always thought I was Jeanne d'Arc and Bonaparte. How little one knows oneself."

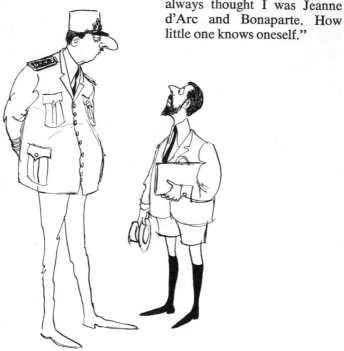

One day the Tall Charles convened a meeting of his "advisors" in Algiers. Though it was a sweltering afternoon, de Gaulle was, as always, dressed with great correctness. One of his younger ministers had the poor judgment to show up in Bermuda shorts. De Gaulle gave him a searing glance: "*Mais, mon petit,* haven't you forgotten your hoop?"

Heckling Hecklers

LONG live hecklers, for they give rise to double delight. In the first place, their jibes are often witty in themselves, and they always bring out doubly witty responses from their targets. I doubt that anything ever advanced the cause of woman suffrage as much as the classic exchange between Emmeline Pankhurst and a heckler. She was addressing a skeptical crowd in Manchester, England, when a wiseacre yelled, "Don't you wish you waz a man?" Emmeline yelled back, "Don't *you* wish you were a man?"

In France, there will always be the legend of the deputy who rose and tried to humiliate a fellow deputy by demanding, "Is it not true that you are actually a veterinary?" Said the second deputy, "Yes, Monsieur— are you ill?"

I suspect it all started with Demosthenes in Athens, when he shouted at General Phocian, "The Athenians will kill you someday when they are in a rage!" Phocian replied, "And they'll kill you someday when they're in their senses."

Anyway, it's fun being in the audience.

Actress Ilka Chase, one of the real wits of the theater world, has a veritable shelf full of books to her credit. One day she ran across Humphrey Bogart at a cocktail party, and he vouchsafed from the corner of his mouth, "Say, baby, that book of yours that just came out—that was a smart job. Who wrote it for you?"

"*I* wrote it," she snapped. "Who read it to you?"

Thomas B. Reed, staunch Republican, was speaking at a rally in Philadelphia, and Democratic hecklers were having a field day. At one point, tempers rose to such a level that a man in the crowd yelled, "Oh, go to hell!"

A hush fell on the gathering, and Mr. Reed made good use of it. "I have given many speeches in Pennsylvania," he said gently, "but this is the first time that my eloquence has won me an invitation to Democratic headquarters."

It sometimes happens that a heckler gets the best of a politician, as when Earl Warren was seeking re-election as Governor of California, and opened his address with "I'm pleased to see such a dense crowd here tonight," and a voice interrupted, "Don't be too pleased, Governor. We ain't all dense."

Lord Beaverbrook, British publishing tycoon, once printed an insulting editorial about a member of Parliament. A few days later, he met the chap in the men's room of a swank London club. "Dear fellow," said Beaverbrook, as he rinsed his hands, "I've been thinking things over, and I feel that the editorial was unjustified. I apologize."

The M.P. graciously accepted.

"But," he added, "next time I'd rather have you insult me in the men's room and apologize in the newspaper!"

In a snide and sarcastic comment about America's multi-racial melting pot, a French literary figure named Paul Bourget once observed to Mark Twain, "When an American has nothing to do, he can always spend a few hours trying to figure out who his grandfather was."

To which Twain replied, "And when all interests fail for a Frenchman, he can always try to find out who his father was, I reckon."

Few squelches are ever as brilliant as the ones we ordinary mortals hatch in bed late at night after the party's over and the chance for retribution irretrievably lost. Unless, of course, one is armed with the golden tongue and the rapier riposte of a Winston Churchill who, in his cups, exuded pearls of pure sarcasm.

Seems that Churchill, wobbly from a bout with brandy, was leaning for support against a marble pillar in a palatial mansion where he had been a dinner guest. A haughty, middle-aged dowager walked up to the careening statesman. "Mr. Churchill, you are drunk," she muttered contemptuously.

"Yes, you are right," agreed Mr. Churchill. "But *you,* madame, are ugly. And in the morning *I* shall be sober."

During a speech in Boston, a heckler interrupted the "silver-tongued" Mayor Jim Curley: "I wouldn't vote for you even if you were Saint Peter."

Curley stared at the man for a moment and said, "Sir, if I were Saint Peter, you wouldn't even be in my district."

95

It happened near a splashy fountain along a pebbly path in the beautifully manicured garden of the Palais de Versailles back in the days of Louis XIV. The snobbish and effeminate Duc de Noailles had gotten the conversation on to his favorite subject: genealogy.

"I can trace my descent in a straight line back to Charlemagne," he sniffed snuffily to the Duc de Dantzig, a newcomer to the Court, who had risen quickly from the lowest origins to the highest royal favor. "Pray, from whom are *you* descended?" lisped the effete Duc de Noailles.

"I am not a descendant," growled the Duc de Dantzig. "I am an ancestor."

When the Republican Senator from New York, Chauncey Depew, introduced Joseph H. Choate at a dinner he said, "Gentlemen, permit me to introduce Ambassador Choate, America's most inveterate after-dinner speaker. All you need to do to Mr. Choate is to open his mouth, drop in a dinner, and up comes a speech."

When Choate rose to speak, he said, "Mr. Depew says that if you open my mouth and drop in a dinner, up will come a speech. But I warn you that if you open your mouths and drop in one of Mr. Depew's speeches, up will come your dinners."

Here's a story that pops up in ad-lib annals so often that I figure it *must* have happened at least once. The last person I've heard it attached to is that indomitable Anglo-American ad-libertine—Lady Astor. The aforesaid lady was making a speech which was continually being interrupted by a disgruntled constituent yelling, "What about the slums of Liverpool?"

Our heroine finally stopped, looked him straight in the eye, and barked, "You're a fit subject for them."

"Take that back! Take that back!" shouted the heckler.

"Very well, I take it back. You are *not* fit for the slums of Liverpool," retorted our Lady.

Guys and Dollars

MARK TWAIN once attended a party where a paunchy tycoon was pontificating on the subject of wealth. "Money is not everything, gentlemen," he said. "It cannot buy happiness, nor can it buy a happy home, nor can it lift the spirits of the saddened, nor alleviate the sufferings of the afflicted, nor buy the love of a good woman."

Said Twain, "You refer, of course, to Confederate money."

Well, it may be true that money isn't everything, but I've discovered it is the subject of a lot of good gags, to wit:

One of Groucho Marx's most celebrated ad-libs was his reply to a Hollywood country club which invited him to join. Said Marx, "I am not interested in joining any organization that would accept me as a member."

Probably Groucho would be surprised to learn that this gag has a noble ancestor. Robert Benchley once lived with his brood in Crestwood, New York. One day, being in his usual need for cash, he went to a local bank where he had a small account and asked for a one-thousand-dollar loan. He was amazed when the bank agreed.

A couple of days later he went and closed out his account. "I've been thinking it over," he explained to a friend, "and I just don't trust a bank that would lend money to such a poor risk as me."

It's hard to sort out the best of Wilson Mizner, his wit was all so good. Mizner, scion of three generations of American diplomats, was determined to become a bum, and he made a brilliant job of it. Most of his friends were swindlers and felons. A burglar friend came to him once and said he was broke. Mizner handed him a fifty-dollar bill with the wry remark, "What's the matter, doesn't it get dark any more?"

To another con man who asked him for a loan of fifty bucks, Mizner said, "Here's twenty-five—let's *both* make twenty-five bucks."

Mizner was a great favorite of many raffish movie stars. Once he was invited to a colossal première at Grauman's Chinese Theatre. The police had to hold back the crowds, which cheered wildly as each sumptuous limousine rolled up and deposited its cargo of glamour. Presently, Mizner rattled to a stop in a broken-down Ford. The crowd gasped. The parking attendant sneered disdainfully as Mizner stepped out. "What shall I do with it, *sir*?"

Mizner, unabashed, handed the keys to the attendant and said, "Keep it."

Even death could not quench his wit. As he lay dying in the hospital, a priest approached his bed. "Thanks, Father," said Mizner, "but I don't need you. In a few minutes I'll be talking with your boss."

James Whistler was often outrageously in debt to the butcher, baker, and candlestick-maker, and he seemed to enjoy the fun of it all. One day he was fortifying himself on fine champagne in a London restaurant, and the director of his tailoring establishment passed by.

"Sir, I should think you'd be ashamed of yourself!" the director exploded. "Here I have been waiting six months for the three hundred pounds you owe, and you sit swilling champagne."

"Oh, don't worry yourself," said Whistler. "I haven't a penny to pay the check."

Ad-libs don't necessarily have to be funny to qualify. They can pack quite a serious message in a few well-chosen, seemingly innocent words. For instance, snobs don't actually have to say, "I'm filthy rich." They just have to respond the way Mrs. Preston Pope Satterwhite did within earshot of Lucius Beebe, author and *bon vivant*. Mr. Beebe had been invited for lunch at the forty-room Fifth Avenue mansion Mrs. Satterwhite had moved into a short time before. The butler interrupted their tête-à-tête to announce that the repast would be served in the Regency Room.

"Where is it?" Mrs. Satterwhite asked.

Art Buchwald reports that one evening he was showing Al Capp around the Pigalle quarter of Paris. A shifty native sidled up to Capp and whispered, "Monsieur wishes to see a feelthy movie?"

Capp, amused, asked, "How much?"

The man said, "Twenty dollar."

Capp yelped, "Twenty dollars for a movie! Who's in it?"

At the Harvard Club in Boston, Novelist John P. Marquand was dallying over a martini when Bernard De Voto entered and asked his advice about a certain fellow writer. "He's asked me to advance him a thousand until he gets his next royalty check."

"Don't do it," said Marquand. "That guy's as broke as the Ten Commandments."

President J. F. Kennedy was exchanging pleasantries with a conservative industrialist at the White House. "You know," mused the Chief Executive, "if I weren't President, I'd be buying stocks now."

"Yes," said the businessman. "And if you weren't President, I'd be buying them too."

Broadway producer Max Gordon is one of the theater's unwitting clowns. Once when he was with a play in Washington, he was invited to a White House dinner by the late Eleanor Roosevelt (who was forever fascinated by his personality). The First Lady introduced Max to an eminent-looking man named Dr. Something-or-Other. Max, who never leaves an opportunity unseized, said, "You know, lately after dinner I have a little burning sensation in my throat ——"

"I'm sorry, Mr. Gordon," interrupted the other. "I am not an M.D.—I am a doctor of economics."

Max hardly batted an eyelash. He said, "Then what looks good on the market, Doc?"

A friend once offered Mark Twain the chance to make a profitable business deal with a merchant whose gains were mostly ill-gotten. "Of course you realize his money's tainted," warned the friend.

"It's twice tainted," corrected Mark Twain. " 'Tain't yours and 'tain't mine."

It happened one spring during the bleak Depression days of the early thirties. A sportswriter sauntered up to Babe Ruth, who was holding out for an eighty-thousand-dollar salary before reporting for spring training with the New York Yankees. "You know, Babe," he said, "that's more money than Herbert Hoover got last year for being President of the United States."

"Uh-huh," said the Bambino, "but I had a better year than Hoover did."

On a trip to Indiana, John D. Rockefeller III was asked at a press conference just how rich the Rockefellers were. He replied, "Well, you could say we have independent means."

Eddie Cantor told me that he was playing in Dallas once with the blond singer Hildegarde. They went shopping at the fabulous Neiman-Marcus department store, and Hildegarde was anxious to buy some pajamas for her uncle. She picked out a style that she liked and asked what they cost.

"Eighty dollars, ma'am," said the clerk.

"*Eighty dollars!*" gasped Hildegarde. "For that money they should come with a man in them!"

After Playwright Moss Hart made a pot of dough out of his *Once in a Lifetime,* he bought a big estate in Pennsylvania that was landscaped within an inch of its life—rows of privet hedges and circles of dwarf pines everywhere. Wolcott Gibbs, of the *New Yorker,* drove down to visit one day, and as he stepped out of the car, Hart asked him what he thought of the place.

"Well," said Gibbs, "it only shows what God could do if he had enough money."

Joe Frisco had a phobia about being robbed. Magazine writer Joe McCarthy tells about the time Frisco checked into a Pittsburgh hotel around midnight and made his usual paranoic search for robbers under the bed, in closets, and behind the window curtains before jumping skittishly into bed. Just for good measure, before pulling the covers up over his head, Frisco called out in a voice that reverberated around the room, "Well, here I am in Pittsburgh, broke again!"

The Classics

IN A roundup of great ad-libs, it is hard to know what to do with the all-time favorites. I have already cited a few here and there, but to print them all would seem a bit superfluous, since everybody knows them already. On the other hand, you can't leave them all out, or people will think *you* don't know them.

For instance, there is the time that Whistler made a brilliant remark at a London club, and Oscar Wilde murmured, "Gad, I wish I'd said that!" Whereupon Whistler reassured him, "Don't worry, Oscar, you will."

This exchange could have taken place, since the two men were contemporaries in London. But it has been attributed to many other wits, so it is hard to say where and when it started.

Another front runner is the exchange between Churchill and Lady Astor about poison and coffee. This we know more about, and there is no doubt at all that it was a fraud. Churchill and Lady Astor were supposed to be in hot debate in Parliament. "Mr. Churchill," cried Lady Astor, "if I were your wife, I would put poison in your coffee." To which Churchill replied, "Madam, if you were my wife, I'd drink it."

Now, Lady Astor and Churchill were never in Parliament at the same time. Moreover, they were very good friends. And furthermore, this joke was current when Winston Churchill was in short pants. It was a favorite in vaudeville; it was even attributed to Umpire Bill Klem in reply to a vociferous lady fan at Ebbetts Field. And it has definitely been traced to the joke pages of college-humor magazines *circa* 1900.

Another supposed Churchill ad-lib goes back even further—to the days he was in his cradle: "An empty taxi drove up to Number Ten Downing Street, and Clement Atlee got out." There is definite proof that it goes back to Aurélian Scholl, a Parisian journalist, who wrote, "An empty hansom cab drove up to the Comédie Française, and Sarah Bernhardt got out."

Somehow, Churchill is mixed up with a lot of classic ad-libs. George Bernard Shaw is supposed to have offered him two seats to the opening of one of his plays. Said Shaw, "Bring a friend—if you have one."

Churchill replied, "I'm sorry that I have a previous engagement, but I'd appreciate tickets for the second night —if you have one."

Churchill's many biographies are good proof that he never met George Bernard Shaw, nor even had any exchange of letters. The second-night gag probably goes back as far as Plautus and Aristophanes.

Shaw himself is given credit for dozens of things that he probably never said. The most famous is his reply to dancer Isadora Duncan, who suggested that they perform a eugenic experiment to produce a child because it would be so wonderful to have a child "with your mind and my body." Shaw declined on the grounds that the child "might have my body and your mind." This is pure bosh, although amusing bosh.

Some ad-libs are a tribute to the human spirit. One windy day, octogenarian Oliver Wendell Holmes was walking down a Washington street with nonagenarian Chauncey Depew when the wind whisked up the skirts of a pretty young pedestrian. Sighed Chief Justice Holmes, "Oh, to be seventy again!"

Some personalities seem to have been especially designed by fate to inspire ad-libs, and it's not always easy to tell why. President Coolidge is an example. Classics sprang up around Cal like daisies, though he was certainly not one of the White House's greatest ornaments. There is the story of the gushing lady reporter who said, "Mr. President, I made a bet with my editor that I could get you to say more than two words."

Said Cal, "You lose."

Another story is that one Sunday morning Mrs. Coolidge was ill, so Cal went to church alone. On his return, Mrs. Coolidge asked, "Calvin, what did the minister preach about?"

"Sin," said Cal.

"And what did he say about sin?" prodded Mrs. Coolidge.

"He was against it."

Dorothy Parker is generally credited with two classics about Coolidge that were originated by two other wits. When Coolidge was elected Vice-President, Alice Roosevelt Longworth remarked, "He looks as though he was weaned on a pickle."

Some years later, newsman Frazier ("Spike") Hunt was told by his managing editor, "Coolidge just died."

Spike asked, "How can they tell?"

Benjamin Disraeli was another classic ad-lib personality, but more understandably so than Coolidge. When asked the difference between a misfortune and a disaster, he said, "Well, if Mr. Gladstone fell into the Thames, that would be a misfortune. But if someone pulled him out, that would be a disaster."

This story has been more recently attributed to Churchill. The truth is that it pre-dated even Disraeli.

Which leads us to the inescapable conclusion that most of the hardy classics are of doubtful origin. They are so apt that they *must* have been said before. So the next time you hear a wit come up with something devastating, perhaps you should not feel too inadequate. Instead of applauding with the remark, "I wish I'd said that," perhaps you should more properly say, "I wish I'd remembered that."

Under-the-Rug Department

THERE COMES a point in every anthology when you find you have a number of items that won't fit into any established category. So you just have to sweep them into a neat pile under the rug and label them miscellaneous. It's at least tidier than the system at Wilson Mizner's old hotel—yes, he was a hotelkeeper among many other things. Mizner's hostelry was a particularly disreputable place near Broadway. To give you a "feel" of the joint, there was a permanent sign in the elevator that read: PLEASE DO NOT SMOKE OPIUM IN THE ELEVATOR.

Mizner provided little or no maid service for his guests. Once a man stalked up to the desk and complained, "My room hasn't been cleaned in a week. What am I going to do about the trash?"

Said Mizner, "Oh, just kick it around till it gets lost."

Which reminds me of disorganization on a loftier plane. When Gauguin and Van Gogh were living and painting together down in Provence, their apartment would never have made the cover of *House Beautiful*. One evening, Van Gogh came home after a hard day's sketching in the fields. "Is there anything to eat?" he asked.

"Yes," said Gauguin, "I think there's a pork chop in the soap dish."

In this spirit, I offer the following soap-dish delicacies:

The first time Henry Ford called on Thomas Edison at his New Jersey home (as he was to do many times again during their long friendship) he found the Edison front gate unusually stubborn. In fact he had to put his weight against it to get through.

"Mr. Edison," said Ford mischievously, "it surprises me that a man of your genius cannot devise a front gate that works more easily."

"Mr. Ford," chuckled the inventor, "that gate is hitched up to my pump—you have just raised me two gallons of water."

While being processed at Fort Meade during the Korean War, William G. Volenick of Baltimore, Maryland, heard a fellow recruit protesting violently to the assignment sergeant who had just earmarked him for the infantry. "But I was a public-relations man in civilian life," the recruit groaned. "You should assign a person to a field where he's had previous experience."

"I'd like to, son," said the old sergeant. "But, you see, the infantry needs men, and not too many come through here who shot people for a living."

Joseph Welch, colorful attorney of the McCarthy hearing, liked to tell a courtroom story in which he got the sharp end of an ad-lib. Welch was defending a man who was accused of brawling with another man and biting part of his ear off. Welch felt pretty well pleased when he got the chief witness to admit that his head was turned away at the moment of the mayhem.

"And so, Mr. Smith," crowed Welch, "you admit that you did not actually *see* the defendant bite the plaintiff's ear off?"

"I did not, sir" responded the witness—and then his face brightened. "But I *did* see him spit it out!"

Groucho Marx, taking a short vacation in Acapulco, Mexico, was introduced to one of the nation's leading bull-fighters. Groucho, fascinated with this branch of show business, drew out the young man, who admitted modestly, "Señor, in my career I have met over a thousand bulls."

"You don't say! I'll bet you're the envy of every cow in Mexico."

Man's blindness to his own faults and follies was never more poignantly expressed than in the words of the great eighteenth-century Scotch poet Robert Burns: "Oh wad some power the giftie gie us to see coursels as others see us." What man cannot see in himself, however, his friends often glimpse all too clearly—and caricaturize all too sharply. I mean by that such ad-lib impressions as Alexander Woollcott's description of his friend, *New Yorker* editor Harold Ross: "He looks like a dishonest Abe Lincoln."

Or sportswriter Hugh Fullerton's off-the-cuff, verbal thumbnail sketch of the cadaverous Ring Lardner: "He looks like Rameses the Second with his wrappings off."

And Neysa MacMein about the unkempt Heywood Broun: "He looks like an unmade bed."

One day Oscar Levant was discussing with a friend the demerits of a California politician who was running for office. "How do you think he'll handle the problem of urban renewal?" the friend asked.

"He'll double-cross that bridge when he comes to it," growled Oscar.

This one is attributed to the famous (or infamous) lawman Wyatt Earp, who was happily officiating at the hanging of a horse thief in Tombstone, Arizona. It was quite a gala event and the entire town was assembled. When Earp asked the horse thief for his last words, he got this response: "I'll tell you how it is, Wyatt. I enjoy a hanging as much as anybody else, but I sure hate to be on this end of the rope."

Which reminds me of the oft-told Lincoln story about the man who was being run out of town on a rail. When a reporter asked the man how he felt about it, he said, "Well, if it wasn't for the honor of the occasion, I'd just as soon have walked."

In search of an apartment some years ago, jazz band-leader and guitarist Eddie Condon ran into a building supervisor who bragged, "In this building we allow no wild parties, children, dogs, musical instruments, or loud radio, hi-fi, or TV playing after eleven at night."

"Fine," said Condon. "But before you accept me as a tenant, there's something I have to tell you: my fountain pen scratches."

Georgie Jessel is a man who has never been known to turn down an invitation to speak, whether the occasion be the investiture of a Supreme Court Justice or the opening of a poolroom. He is in constant demand for funeral orations, which he delivers with convincing emotion.

One day, at Campbell's funeral parlor in New York, he was delivering a eulogy of wondrous eloquence over the bier of a small-time actor: "As he leaves this world, he takes a small part of the heart of everyone who knew him. Few of us can forget the wonderful spirit of this great friend who . . ."

Georgie looked down fondly at the open casket, and suddenly drew back in surprise. "My God, I *know* this man!"

Franklin P. Adams mentioned between card-game deals at the Algonquin Hotel one night that he had seen an incredible sight earlier in the day—Harold Ross (oddball editor of the *New Yorker* magazine) tobogganing.

"Good Lord! Ross tobogganing!" exclaimed George S. Kaufman. "Did he look funny?"

"Well," Adams said, "you know how he looks *not* tobogganing."

And no aficionado of bons mots should ever forget F.P.A.'s brilliant pun when someone remarked during the Spanish Civil War that the only way for enemies of Franco to be smuggled out of Spain was through the Basque country.

"Yes," said F.P.A., "the Spaniards are putting all their Basques in one exit."

One afternoon a young lady admirer of James Whistler innocently asked the great painter whether he thought genius was hereditary. She was startled by the reply; "I can't tell, madam. Heaven has granted me no offspring."

Fate usually accords every man the opportunity to make at least one outrageous pun in his lifetime. Some men make a great show of shunning puns as "the lowest form of humor." But Sir James Barrie, author of *Peter Pan,* was not contra-puntal.

"Sir James," an acquaintance asked him one day, "have all your plays been successes?"

"Oh, no," said Barrie. "Some Peter out and others Pan out."

Early in his career as Governor of New York, Al Smith, on an inspection visit to Sing Sing Prison, was asked by the warden to deliver a short speech to the inmates. Still lacking forensic finesse, Al unthinkingly addressed the assembled convicts as "my fellow citizens." This unleashed a slight titter among the yardbirds, who were painfully aware that, as inmates of a penitentiary, they were no longer citizens. Realizing his mistake, the rookie Governor began again. "My fellow convicts," he intoned, and then bit his tongue as laughter swept through the auditorium. Completely flustered by now Smith made his third, and perhaps most ill-fated attempt to get his speech off the ground. "Well, anyway, I'm glad to see so many of you here," said he.

When Edna Ferber and George Kaufman were collaborating on the hit play, *Dinner at Eight,* much of the work was done in Miss Ferber's room at the Hotel Algonquin. The hotel's famed proprietor, Frank Case, was an unusually moralistic man (for a hotelkeeper), and he made no exceptions even for his celebrated guests. Once, at 2:30 A.M., he phoned Miss Ferber's room and asked, "Do you have a gentleman in your room?"

"I don't know," she said. "Wait a minute and I'll ask him."

Short and Not So Sweet

By AND LARGE, I think the best ad-libs of all are the mini-libs—the ones that pack everything into two or three words. They're like the mustard on a hot dog, the olive in a martini. Here are my nominations, but I don't suppose anyone will ever quite equal General Mac-Aulliffe's famous retort, "Nuts!," when the German High Command demanded that he surrender in the Battle of the Bulge.

Newspapermen have an uncanny habit of asking famous people to give their secret of success "in three words." When an interviewer challenged Bernard Baruch to capsule the secret of longevity in three words, he responded, "Choose healthy parents."

Architect Frank Lloyd Wright also fielded the three-word query flawlessly. To the question, "What is the best foundation for a house?" he answered, "A happy couple."

That great sportswriter-naturalist John Kieran (who will go down in history as the man who said, "I was born of poor but Irish parents") was arguing an ornithological point with zoologist Roger Conant. "Dammit, John," said Conant, "I can't argue with you. Why is it that you Irishmen always answer a question by *asking* one?"

John widened his eyes innocently. "Do we?"

Veteran press agent Dick Maney was once hired by a new producer to tub-thump for his first Broadway play. During the tryout, Maney realized that the show would be murdered by the critics. The day the show opened in New York, the producer was worrying about whether he should wear a dinner jacket for the opening. He approached Maney and said, "Dick, I don't know the tradition—what suit do you think I should wear?"

Maney snapped, "Your track suit."

The craggy-faced Richard Boone is also famous for his rather craggy, no-nonsense disposition. Once a gushy girl reporter from a fan magazine asked, "Mr. Boone, after so many years of appearing in Western pictures, how do you feel toward your horse?"

Boone squared his jaw and said, "Distant."

In spite of their seeming diversity, the late Jack Teagarden (top jazz trombonist) and Willie McCovey (top first baseman) had one important trait in common—they loved to sleep.

When a reporter asked Jack why it was that he liked to sleep so long every day, Jack thought it over and said, "Maybe it's because I sleep *slow.*"

In the case of Willie McCovey, a California sports editor phoned his hotel at 10 A.M. to check an important story. When a sleepy voice answered, the editor said, "Sorry, Willie—did I wake you up?"

Said Willie, "Some."

One day in a conversation with Oscar Wilde, Welsh poet Lewis Morris bemoaned the fact that the press never published any of his work.

"It's a conspiracy of silence, Oscar. What should I do?"

"Join it," said Oscar.

When violinist Yehudi Menhuin made his debut at Carnegie Hall as a boy prodigy (1923), violinist Mischa Elman and pianist Alexander Brailowsky sat next to each other in a box. Young Menhuin, dressed in knee breeches, had just breezed through a devilishly difficult Paganini passage, and Elman wiped his brow. "Don't you think it's a little warm in here?" he whispered.

Brailowsky whispered back, "Not for piano players!"

Jimmy Durante, whose mastery of golf does not quite measure up to either his nose or his prose, was trudging dejectedly off the eighteenth green after playing a calamitous round with his old vaudeville partner, Lou Clayton. "What should I give the caddy?" Durante asked.

"Your clubs," Clayton shot back.

Franklin P. Adams, the great and crusty columnist, hated bores beyond everything else. One night at the Players Club, a pompous character embarked on a funny story and got bogged down in the middle. "Well," he said lamely, "to make a long story short . . ."

"Too late!" snapped Adams.

Perhaps another of F.P.A.'s remarks is too loquacious to qualify for this chapter, but I'll include it anyway. At the Lambs Club, F.P.A. got into an argument with a well-hated chap whom we shall call Charlie. Charlie flew into a rage and stalked off in high dudgeon. One of the old-timers clucked his tongue: "That Charlie is his own worst enemy!" F.P.A. rumbled, "Not while I'm around!"

When asked by a reporter how many people work in the Vatican, Pope John XXII answered good-naturedly, "About half!"

Hollywood's Harry Cohn once assumed his seat at the head of the table and announced, "Gentlemen, I am going to England next week."

Norman Krasna, at the end of the table, took the cue immediately: "Gee, Mr. Cohn, can I go along with you?"

Cohn stared down the table scornfully. "Go with me!" he snorted. "Now, why on earth would I take a punk like you to England with me?"

"As interpreter."

When Henry Thoreau lay dying in his home, a relentlessly pious neighbor paid a bedside call and asked primly, "Henry, have you made your peace with God?"

Thoreau whispered, "We never quarreled."

"Let them eat cake" and *"Après moi, le déluge"* were not the only ad-libs attributable to French monarchs. For instance, when Louis XIII was on his deathbed his last wish was that his yóung son be brought to him. When the boy arrived, the King looked at him lovingly and, in the manner of fathers everywhere, asked, "What is your name, son?"

"Louis XIV," was the reply.

"Not yet," snapped the King.

James Thurber used to delight in reminiscing about his grandfather, who was one of the most renowned Indian fighters of his day. When the doughty old man was on his deathbed, the preacher asked him if he had made peace with his enemies. "Don't have any," he replied.

"Amazing," said the preacher. "Pray, tell me how you've managed to live so long without making enemies?"

"I shot 'em."

And now, as the sun sinks slowly behind the lovely hills of Ad-Libia, I should like to point out a humble headstone in the churchyard of a tiny English village called Whitchurch. The stone marks the grave of a man who, even unto death, was faithful to the spirit of ad-libs — particularly short ad-libs. His name was McGinnis, and his stone reads simply: FINIS MCGINNIS. I never knew Mr. McGinnis in this life, but I feel such a close kinship that if I ever run across him in the hereafter, I shall be tempted to hail him:

FINIS!